THE DIARIO

THE DIARIO

THE DARING ESCAPE
OF TWO SEPHARDIC JEWS
FROM TURKEY TO AMERICA
DURING WORLD WAR I

Written in Ladino by
Alfred Ascher

Translated & Introduced by
Gloria J. Ascher

Albion
Andalus
Boulder, Colorado
2023

"The old shall be renewed,
and the new shall be made holy."
— Rabbi Avraham Yitzhak Kook

Albion-Andalus Inc.
P. O. Box 19852
Boulder, CO 80308
albionandalus.com

Design and composition by Albion-Andalus Books

Cover design by Hauke Storm

ISBN-13 (Paperback): 978-1-953220-29-5

ISBN-13 (Hardcover): 978-1-953220-30-1

Manufactured in the United States of America

A mis keridos tíos Alfred i Albert,
mi kerido suvrino Bobby (Robert),
i mi kerido padre Emanuel Ascher,
todos de bindicha memoria,
ke me azen deynda sunriyir

To my dear uncles Alfred and Albert,
my dear cousin Bobby (Robert),
and my dear father Emanuel Ascher,
all of blessed memory,
who still make me smile

FAMIYA (FAMILY)

A mi tío Alfred, de bindicha memoria:

Enfin tu Diario está saliendo
al mundo, en inglés también!
En mizmo tiempo está reuniendo
muestra famiya—saves ken?
Inyetos de Albert! I otros Ascheres
del mundo entero! Ke alegría!
Sunriyir te veo por los buenos haberes!
Ke todos ke lo meldan se agan famiya!

To my Uncle Alfred, of blessed memory:

Finally your Diary is coming out
into the world, in English, too!
It's also reuniting our family—
They're writing to me—you know who?
Albert's grandchildren! And other Aschers
all over the world! What a pleasure!
I see you smiling down at us!
May all become family who read this treasure!

Acknowledgements

Grasias!—thank you to everyone who helped make this edition of Alfred Ascher's *Diario* a reality, notably:

Matilda Koén-Sarano, who encouraged and enabled me to reclaim my ancestral language—a prerequisite for this endeavor!

Prof. Asta Helena Lepinis, of blessed memory, who appreciated the value of the *Diario* and pushed persistently for its publication.

My Ascher cousins: David, Allen, Wendy and Paul Ascher, grandchildren of Albert, for sharing family lore and photos; Perla Vida Asher Samuels, Hayim Danon, Leah Teicher, Izyk Ascher, and Avner Sidi of the Roots-Ascher WhatsApp group for documenting, sharing, interpreting, and continuing our family history and traditions; and Perla Vida Asher Samuels, Zvi Samuels and Izyk Ascher for help in sharing and locating photos.

Prof. Jane Mushabac, for her inspiration and example—her novel, *His Hundred Years, A Tale* by Shalach Manot (nom de plume), was beautifully presented by Albion-Andalus Books—and for her continuing support, advice, efforts, and encouragement, from the very beginning.

Rachel Amado Bortnick, native Izmirli, for her invaluable help with both geographical and historical/cultural questions, and for the appropriate photo of Smyrna.

Members of the Ladinokomunita, for their generous help in solving linguistic and other problems.

Rashelika Cohen, for sharing good ideas, translating Greek expressions, and, together with dogs Ollie and Duckie, facilitating recreational breaks.

Prof. Devin Naar, for sharing generously his extensive knowledge and expertise, his writings and other sources, which helped illuminate historical and cultural contexts.

Liliana Benveniste, for her persistent, thoughtful, and creative efforts to identify Greek islands.

Francis Moïsi and Monica (Berger) Moïsi, for sharing their experience interpreting, evaluating, and presenting family treasures: Holocaust-era letters (Monica) and a miniature Sefer Torah (Francis), and for encouraging and inspiring me by their example.

Emma Youcha, for their support, encouragement, and advice, and for their precious gift: a German map of Smyrna engraved in 1895, three years after Alfred was born—a magical portal into his world.

Prof. Dina Danon, a historian with both roots and professional expertise in Izmir's Jewish community, for her presentation and explanation of valuable pertinent sources.

Members of my Explore Ladino! group (Zoom), for their support, encouragement, good wishes, and refreshing diversion.

Yvonne Igoe, for her continuing encouragement and support, and for her practical help in submitting the original manuscript of the *Diario* to Albion-Andalus Books years ago, when I was in rehab.

Dr. Dov Pine, whose witty prodding (in Ladino) helped propel the completion of this project.

Dr. David Leaf, for sharing his experience and advice as an author.

Netanel Miles-Yépez of Albion-Andalus Books, who recognized the worth of the *Diario* and agreed to publish it.

Daniel Jami of Albion-Andalus Books, my editor, whose expertise and challenging engagement with the text helped improve the final product.

I grasias al Dio for enabling us to reach this precious moment! *Sheeheyanu!*

CONTENTS

Foreword   1

Introduction   3

Preface to the *Diario*   26

Diario: Part I   28

Diario: Part II   60

Foreword

My father's native language was Ladino. My mother grew up speaking Yiddish. Neither language was spoken at home. I am, as my wife put it, the product of a linguistic mixed marriage. I learned Spanish in school and hence was able to read some of my father's diary. But I was baffled by many words and phrases. Luckily, we have a Ladino scholar in the family—my cousin Gloria Ascher. She agreed to tackle the diary, and I, our extended family, and those who read her knowledgeable and inspired translation are forever indebted to her and are grateful for her efforts on our behalf.

It is now common to celebrate one's roots. This was not the case fifty years ago. My parents were intent on raising their children to be complete Americans; the past, their past, they kept largely to themselves. Growing up, I did not know where my father was born and lived his youth. I found out by chance.

In the spring of 1965 I was preparing to participate in an excavation in Turkey at the ancient Lydian site of Sardis. In a brief telephone conversation, I casually mentioned my plans to my father. Just as casually, he said that he was born and grew up in Izmir, about sixty miles from Sardis, and that his brother Haim still lived there. About an hour later, my wife and I telephoned again and offered to finance a trip that would enable him to travel to Izmir. He accepted our offer.

We all met at Haim's apartment in Izmir: Haim and his wife and daughter; my father and his brother Emanuel (Gloria's father), who had also settled in the U.S. and taken the trip with him; and us. After dinner, fueled by raki, we went out into the street and did a line dance. My father and all of his brothers and sisters have since died. With the publication of the diary, may the dance go on.

Robert Ascher
Emeritus Professor of Anthropology
Cornell University

Introduction

Welcome to the world of Alfred Ascher's *Diario*! It is a world full of adventure and danger, mystery and surprises, reflecting problems like mutual stereotyping, antisemitism, and the plight of refugees and immigrants—relevant in our challenging times, as in all times. There are also hints of solutions—traits, attitudes, and values that are ever relevant as well. To make this extraordinary work accessible to the widest possible audience, it is presented here in a bilingual edition, in the original Ladino with a side-by-side English translation, designed for both the general reader and the student and scholar. Ideally, the reader's first encounter with this work (indeed, with any work worth knowing) should be as direct as possible, unencumbered by extraneous information and others' interpretations, however valuable. But the nature of the *Diario*, its language and its historical, cultural and personal context, demands commentary. So, in order to facilitate and maximize the reader's understanding and appreciation of this work and its significance, it is presented together with introductory and explanatory materials. Still, the reader is urged not to continue reading this introduction before savoring a bit of the *Diario* itself, thus assuring a direct, personal first encounter.

Written by Alfred Ascher, a Sephardic Jew born in Smyrna, now Izmir, Turkey in 1892, the *Diario* in the original Ladino is presented here in a typed version, together with a facsimile of some original pages of the only known manuscript, a photocopy consisting of sixty handwritten pages plus a handwritten title page. The typed version aims to be as faithful

as possible to the letter as well as the spirit of the original, and thus, for example, preserves characteristic inconsistencies in spelling. But some changes have been made to insure clarity, readability, appropriate presentation, and correspondence between the original and the translation. Obvious slips of the pen have been corrected. Commas have often been replaced by periods in accordance with common usage. Some paragraphs have been created or adjusted. Quotation marks have replaced the misleading parentheses used to indicate foreign words and special expressions. At first undertaken reluctantly, these changes are actually a means of fulfilling the complex, gradually unfolding nature and purpose of the *Diario*.

Our first introduction to the *Diario* is the title page, which presents the original, formal, ambitious, and impressive full title and subtitle: *Diario de Mi Viajé en 2 Partes. Smyrna to New York, August 10th, 1915 – December 25th, 1915: Inolvidalves i Esmovientes Passajes (Diary of My Journey in 2 Parts . . . Unforgettable and Moving Passages)*. The fancy, almost calligraphic script heightens the impression of formality. Though the narrative that follows consists of only sixty small, handwritten notebook pages, it is divided into two beautifully labelled 'parts,' preceded by a short preface. This formal, structured presentation suggests that Alfred viewed the *Diario* as something precious that should be fittingly presented to the world. The changes in the original noted above honor this intention and should help insure its realization.

Yet it is clear from the preface and comments interspersed in the narrative that the *Diario* is addressed foremost to Alfred's family, the 'dear ones' he and his brother Albert left behind in Smyrna. It is, on one level, Alfred's long, intimate, extended letter to them, which he closes with the flourish of his signature. It is thus appropriate that the *Diario* is being presented to a wider audience by members of his family. Alfred Ascher was my uncle, and the manuscript was given to me, the Ladino speaker in the family, by his son Robert, who graciously agreed to write

the foreword to this edition. He discovered it among possessions left by his sister, Lorraine Lonstein, after her death in 1996. My Aunt Nelly, the widow of Alfred's youngest brother, Haim, and her daughter, Rosie, both of whom, like Alfred, were born in Smyrna/Izmir, generously shared their knowledge of Turkish expressions and locations in the *Diario*. Yet nobody in the surviving family seemed to know that such a *Diario* existed— until Lorraine's son William Lonstein contacted his uncle Robert Ascher, asking to see Alfred's account of his trip to this country! William's memory of his mother mentioning such an account was sparked by his teenage son, who, while watching the 2012 Summer Olympics, asked about their family's roots. The curiosity of Alfred's great-grandson thus reawakened in his grandson the memory of the *Diario*'s existence.

More recently, Albert's grandchildren, David, Allen, Wendy and Paul Ascher, have shared memories and family stories relating to some of the *Diario*'s mysteries, like the time it was written. Towards the end of the narrative, Alfred mentions that Albert had gotten married and that he too would soon be married, indicating that the *Diario* was completed in 1920, between March 25th and April 17th. David remembers visiting Alfred in Lorraine's apartment in Worcester, Massachusetts, probably in August 1979, and hearing Alfred tell stories of his journey. He also remembers hearing Lorraine say that her father had written down some of his stories, and that she was urging him to finish recording them. This would indicate that at least part of the *Diario* was written over fifty years later! But the *Diario* recounts past experiences and events in amazing and precise detail, sometimes approaching a day-to-day record, a 'diary' in the literal sense—an unlikely fruit of old memories alone!

The narrative is lively, peppered by wit and humor, and at the same time, presented from the perspective of the writer's feelings at the time of writing. Interwoven with past events and present emotions are also hopes and prospects for the

future. Alfred may have written portions in or before 1920 and completed it years later, perhaps using old notes. This would help explain its complex nature, as both an intimate letter to his family and a formal memoir for the world.Whatever the chronology of its composition, the *Diario* is a convincing, integrated whole. Its preface opens with Alfred's overwhelming feeling that he can neither write nor explain his departure to those he left behind; Part I proceeds with his narration of past events—"It was on the morning of ...;" and Part II ends with his hope of seeing them all again. Within this framework, past experiences, present feelings and future hopes are interwoven throughout the richly textured account.

Albert's grandchildren, together with members of the Ascher family WhatsApp group, have also helped shed light on other problematic aspects of the *Diario*. At various pivotal points in the narrative, Alfred refers to himself and Albert as "Frenchmen." Like my father, who was proud of his French identity, Alfred and Albert were French citizens or 'subjects.' They may have acquired this identity under the commercially motivated capitulation agreements between the Ottoman Empire and European countries, like France. But according to family lore as recalled by his grandson David, Albert was born in Algiers, as were both his parents. In that case, they would already have been French citizens before emigrating to Smyrna: the Crémieux decree of 1870 granted French citizenship to all Jews born in Algeria, which was then under French rule. But it s unclear whether their French citizenship would have been recognized by the Ottoman Empire. It is also unclear whether the French citizenship of Albert's father would have been extended to Alfred and his younger siblings, who were born in Smyrna to a different mother.

According to the recollection of Albert's grandchildren, this French identity that both brothers so prized was the main reason they left Smyrna; for as French citizens they would have been considered 'enemy aliens' by the Ottoman regime, now

fighting in World War I on the side of Germany and against the Allied Forces that included France. As the two eldest sons, Albert and Alfred were of military age and feared they might be imprisoned—or worse. Though the *Diario* itself gives no such concrete, specific reason for their departure, Alfred concludes his preface with the statement that he "did it in order to escape once and for all from the hand of this 'Barbarous Turk.'" This is startling in view of my family's generally positive view of Turks as kind and welcoming. We are, after all, descendants of the Jews expelled from Spain in 1492 who found refuge and a life of relative prosperity in the Ottoman Empire. So much of our culture has been enriched by Turkish influence; we even call ourselves 'Turkinos'!

The stereotype of the 'Barbarous Turk' or 'Terrible Turk' has its origins in medieval European perceptions of the Saracens, and the expression itself finds echoes in Chaucer and Shakespeare, and was used by such different personages as Voltaire, Thomas Hood, and Henry Morgenthau. It became common in the early 20th century (and even beyond). At that time—the time of the *Diario*—Turkey was involved in multiple wars, becoming responsible for thousands of deaths, as well as for what is now recognized as the Armenian genocide. Though Jews were not specifically targeted, they were certainly aware of what was happening, and many expressed their horror. Alfred's use of the stereotypical expression should be understood in this context. He was also no doubt aware of happenings that, while less gruesome, were nonetheless devastating and closer to home.

According to my cousin Izyk Ascher, the Ottoman regime at that time pressured, in effect forced, Jews to 'donate' to the war effort, in gratitude for having been so well received after their expulsion from Spain over four hundred years before. One of these Jews was our relative Yosef Ascher (1844-1918). As a result, this talented, versatile, and successful entrepreneur, merchant and community leader and benefactor, who had renounced his French citizenship in order to participate in

Smyrna municipal affairs, lost his well-earned fortune and died broken and depressed. With all this as context, Alfred, as if to illustrate the last words of his preface, later relates his personal encounter with the 'Barbarous Turk': the haunting, "horrible" devastation he witnesses on the deserted island Anglo Nissi/ English Adassi, "all done by the Turks."

At least as essential for understanding the *Diario* as this historical, cultural and personal context is its language. The *Diario* is written in the language commonly known as Ladino, referred to as (Eastern) Judeo-Spanish by scholars, and simply called *Spanyol* (Spanish) or *Spanyol de mozotros* (our Spanish) by native speakers of Alfred Ascher's family and community. Spoken by descendants of Jews expelled from Spain in 1492 who settled in the Ottoman Empire, Ladino is based on 15th-century Castilian Spanish. At first glance, it sounds and reads like modern Spanish, and it does remain close to its sister language; but it is a distinct language in its own right, with various dialects. Even before the expulsion from Spain, Ladino was enriched by elements of Hebrew (it's a Jewish language!), Aramaic and Greek, which the Jews had brought with them, and Arabic, the primary language of Spanish lands during the centuries of Muslim rule (711-1492 C.E.). In the course of its development, Ladino has been further enriched by the languages and cultures of the various places of resettlement, notably the lands of the Ottoman Empire, and more recently, Turkey, Israel, France, and the USA.

The influence of two of these languages is evident in the title of the *Diario*. The spelling of '*viajé*' with the *accent aigu* over the 'e' reflects the French influence that pervades the text. Such influence can be seen in the use of accents (the *accent grave* and the *cédille* in addition to the *accent aigu*), the spelling of Judeo-Spanish words, and the abundance of words, phrases, and even whole sentences in French. Though the inclusion of French in the *Diario* is related, in part, to the events of the narrative, the influence of the French language is also a result of the author

having attended a school in his native Smyrna established by the Allliance Israélite Universelle, which aimed to educate Jewish children throughout the Middle East in the ways of 'modern,' that is, French civilization. The French influence became common among Turkish Sefaradim of that time, and likely contributed to the negative view that Alfred, as a French-educated person, expresses of uneducated people, like some of the Turks and Greeks he encounters.

The second part of the title, *Smyrna to New York, August 10th, 1915 – December 25th, 1915*, is entirely in English. Though he arrived in this country with no knowledge of English, Alfred had, in the intervening five to fifty plus years, obviously made the language of his new home his own. Indeed, the Judeo-Spanish of the *Diario* is enlivened by sudden, startling outbursts of American English words and phrases, which are rendered in italics in the English translation. Even the spelling and vocabulary of the Ladino are sometimes influenced by English.

Nonetheless, Spanish provides the dominant linguistic flavor, and often seems to determine spelling; though the same word, at different points, is sometimes spelled not only as it is in Spanish, but also as it is in French, English, and phonetic Judeo-Spanish transcription. Spanish forms seem to be accepted as normative, as more 'correct,' like 'Dios' (God), which appears more often than the usual Judeo-Spanish 'Dio.'

Turkish, Greek, and Hebrew elements are less frequent. Turkish and Greek place names and specialized words and expressions, sometimes modified, occur naturally in the narrative. Alfred refers to himself twice as *"el tchilibi de Efraim,"* the gentleman Efraim, both times in humorous situations. The humor inherent in this telling self-designation stems from the combination and juxtaposition of the Turkish term for an educated, cultured gentleman (*tchilibi*) and Alfred's Hebrew name (Efraim). The Hebrew elements in the *Diario* are few in number, but their implications for the author are unmistakable. The diminutive form of his Hebrew name, Efraimico (p.56-7),

suggests intimacy—the *Diario* is, after all, addressed to his family—and an awareness of his Jewish identity.

Exploring the influences of various languages reveals another feature that characterizes the richly textured Judeo-Spanish of the *Diario*: inconsistencies in spelling and usage, resulting in multiple forms. A striking example are the place names given in different languages or in combinations of languages, one form occurring close to or even directly following another. For example, the island Anglo Nissi is also called English Adassi, Inglis adasi, and Ingless adassi, all meaning English Island, with 'island' rendered in both Greek (*nissi*) and Turkish (*adassi*). There is meaning behind the use of multiple forms, of the almost systematic inconsistencies that define and enliven the language of the *Diario*. In the case of the now Turkish island currently called Ingiliz Adasi, the meaning is painfully clear from the brief historical context and graphic description Alfred presents. The conscious, overt use of such forms thus reflects the author's recognition that there are many forms that can not only exist in a language, but can coexist in the same work, and that each form is indeed valid, worthy of mention, loaded with meaning, and connected to the others.

The *Diario* is thus written in a Judeo-Spanish that sparkles with the flavors of French, American English, Spanish, Turkish, Greek, and Hebrew, going beyond expectation even for a language that is characteristically enriched by the pronounced influence of other languages. Phrases and complete sentences in English, French, and Greek appear suddenly, often at pivotal points in the narrative. The language of the *Diario* is further enriched (and complicated) by the noted inconsistencies, the abundance of multiple forms.

Rendering such a text into English for the scholarly and general reader alike presents special problems. First of all, how can words from other languages best be 'translated'? As previously noted, borrowings from American English are printed in italics to mark them as part of the original text. As

for words and phrases in other languages, some are left in the original for flavor, though sometimes in transcription that has been modified to facilitate pronunciation. They are presented in quotation marks, with translations and brief explanations in the text or in notes. Other such words and phrases are translated into English where there is a clear equivalent, in order to facilitate immediate comprehension, even at the expense of flavor. Another challenge is the repetitive nature of the *Diario's* vocabulary, which necessitates different translations of the same word, depending on context, in order to insure clarity and naturalness of expression in English. Yet another problem is posed by the syntax, which is typically a series of clauses, one building on the other, referring back or ahead, and propelling the narrative to a climax. Some passages consist of many clauses connected by '*i* (and),' reminiscent of the Hebrew scriptures. While this narrative technique can be very effective in the original Judeo-Spanish, it tends to merely create tedious run-on sentences in English. I have therefore adjusted the syntax in order to transpose both the import and the excitement of the original Ladino.

Though a worthy work in its own right, as a Ladino document the *Diario* has special significance. According to UNESCO (The United Nations Educational, Scientific and Cultural Organization), Ladino is a "severely endangered" language, with about 150,000 speakers. At the same time, it is a flourishing living language that has been enjoying a world-wide resurgence, accelerated in response to the COVID-19 pandemic. There is now a veritable cornucopia, an explosion of activities using the latest technology, initiated and powered by activists of diverse backgrounds, and often produced by groups working together. There are presentations, meetings, and classes in the language, including my own, which are bringing together participants of all ages and backgrounds from around the world and creating a wonderful new sense of community. The following sampling of pioneering initiatives to promote Ladino, dating from the 1990's to today, is taken from my experience and, though by no means

exhaustive, should give the reader some idea of the wealth and vibrancy of the current resurgence in which the *Diario* partakes.

First and foremost are the efforts and achievements of Matilda Koén-Sarano, the *grande dame* of Ladino. Based in Israel, she was urged by her father, Alfredo Sarano, to use her talents to save the language, which he saw was in danger. Matilda has become the prime advocate, activist, poet, scholar, author, dramatist, lyricist, teller and collector of folktales, and creator of cookbooks, crossword puzzles, textbooks and dictionaries in Ladino, exemplifying the power and breadth of its continuing resurgence.

Although there is no geographic community where Ladino is the primary language, there are now multiple virtual communities. The longest lasting is the *Ladinokomunita*, founded in January 2000 by Rachel Amado Bortnick, which has attracted around 1,500 members from many countries. We correspond exclusively in Ladino, sharing news and experiences, videos and articles, original poems and sketches, and commenting on a seemingly infinite variety of subjects— including problematic names, words and passages in the *Diario*.

The journal *Aki Yerushalayim (Jerusalem Here)*, entirely in Judeo-Spanish, is in its forty-fourth year of publication, with only a two-year hiatus. It now appears solely online, with a new editorial team headed by Aldo Sevi. It was founded by Moshe Shaul, of blessed memory, a great champion of Ladino, and my relative, born in Izmir. Moshe also proposed the idea that became the *Ladinokomunita*, and devised the now widely-accepted system of writing Ladino phonetically in Roman letters.

El Amaneser (The Dawn), the monthly periodical entirely in Ladino (Karen Gerson Şarhon, editor-in-chief; Güler Orgun, co-editor), has been published for over eighteen years in Istanbul as a distinctive and independent 'supplement' to the weekly newspaper Şalom, which itself includes one or two pages in Judeo-Spanish. *El Amaneser* alone has attracted almost 150

subscribers for the printed edition and more than 300 online, in addition to those who receive it together with *Şalom*. In October 2021, the special 200th issue of *El Amaneser* appeared, containing forty-eight instead of the usual twenty-four pages, but some contributions still had to be published later for an encouraging reason—there was no room left!

Thanks to Liliana and Marcelo Benveniste, based in Argentina, Ladino enthusiasts by the hundreds have been coming for over three years to enjoy the *Enkontros de Alhad*: Sunday gatherings on Zoom with conversations in Judeo-Spanish—and now sometimes in Haketia (Western Judeo-Spanish) as well as in the usual Ladino—between featured 'hosts' and a variety of 'guests,' from Matilda Koén-Sarano to notable singers, scholars, writers, activists, and . . . me! A recent guest was Juan Sanchez Guerra, who started learning Ladino five years ago, when he was 13, and thus represents a new generation of Ladino speakers and activists. Personal interaction is encouraged through comments and questions in the chat, which are read aloud or otherwise conveyed to the 'guest,' helping to create the feel of a family get-together. All *Enkontros* are recorded and available on YouTube.

Notable among the many classes on Zoom offered by the Sephardic Jewish Brotherhood of America is Albert Maimon's reading and discussion of the Ladino religious classic *Meam Loez*. Special for me was Rabbi Nissim Elnecavé's class *Sephardic Siddur and Liturgy*, where I learned to sing, among other treasures, the Ladino grace after meals. In April 2022, Rabbi Elnecavé shared his talents and our music and language with a wider audience, at Carnegie Hall! In addition to selections in Hebrew, he sang two liturgical and religious pieces and a song/poem by a woman from Rhodes who survived Auschwitz—all three in Ladino!

There are new poems, songs, musical comedies, plays, and stories being written in Ladino, as well as cookbooks and dictionaries (most recently, for speakers of Hebrew and Turkish). At least four memoirs in Ladino have been published,

and there are three Ladino textbooks available in English alone. The living Judeo-Spanish language is being taught to new generations from diverse ethnic and religious backgrounds, who become enthusiastic transmitters of the language and culture.

Thankfully, such passionate learners have been among my students at Tufts University, where I offered a basic course on Ladino Language and Culture every semester from January 2000 to May 2017 to meet the demand, with continuation courses on request. Exemplary of such passion is my current FaceTime student, who began learning Ladino as a Tufts senior, and has continued, with unparalleled enthusiasm and motivation, since graduation. And now I even have a wonderful new student in Australia who sought me out. Such is the attraction and power of this language! My Ladino sessions on Zoom, which started in December 2020 and continue to welcome new participants, have attracted students and professors, musicians and composers, native speakers and beginners, Jews of various backgrounds and persuasions, Muslims and Christians, and people who have lived from one to ninety-one years.

Bryan Kirschen has pioneered creative ways of learning and teaching the language, from ucLADINO (as a graduate student) to the Ladino Collaboratory (as a professor at SUNY Binghamton). The Endangered Language Alliance (Ross Perlin) has produced a variety of detailed and thoughtfully conceived videos showcasing Ladino speakers, singers, and storytellers of various generations and backgrounds (including me), in a near-natural environment, presented complete with transcription and English translation on YouTube. The recent Ladino course offered at Oxford by Carlos Yebra López attracted more students than could be accommodated. Courses in Ladino are offered at the University of Pennsylvania by Daisy Sadaka Braverman, and in the spring of 2023 Ladino was introduced at Harvard. Funded by the University of Karlstad, Sweden, for two years beginning in 2022, Kent Fredholm is conducting telephone and

Zoom interviews of Ladino teachers and learners worldwide, in order to identify possibilities, difficulties, and needs.

There is a new generation of singers and composers, like Lily Henley and Tutti Druyan, eager to learn Ladino in order to perform the traditional songs responsibly and incorporate them into their broader projects. From among the new songs being composed in Ladino, whole albums have been created for children, like those by Sarah Aroeste. Children, notably the choir *Las Estreyikas d'Estanbol* (The Little Stars of Istanbul), founded by Izzet Bana, are being taught to sing in Ladino. A book created for children, *Romances de la Rata Sabia* by Paloma Díaz-Mas (2021), was translated from the original Spanish into Ladino (*Romansas de la Ratona Savia*) by a group led by Rachel Amado Bortnick and Rina Benmayor. Our lively, often heated but incredibly fruitful, Ladino discussions on Zoom attest to the vibrancy of the language.

Collections of Judeo-Spanish proverbs and tales abound, as do relevant scholarly studies, conferences, and academic programs. There are several research centers devoted to Judeo-Spanish language and culture, from Istanbul to Seattle to Be'er Sheva. Documents in Ladino are being discovered and preserved, including online, notably through the initiative of Devin Naar at the University of Washington. International Ladino Day, first proposed by Zelda Ovadia to Israel's National Authority for Ladino and Its Culture, has been celebrated since 2013 across the globe, from Jerusalem to Buenos Aires, from Istanbul to Madrid, and, in the U.S. alone, from Boston to Dallas to New York (thanks to creator/founder Jane Mushabac), and from Seattle to Elon, North Carolina (through the initiative of Judith Lin).

Exemplified and nurtured by such activities, interest in Ladino has grown even more dramatically since November 2021, when Netflix began distributing the Turkish film series *Kulüp* (*The Club*). This series, which portrays the plight of Sephardic Jews in 1950s Turkey, contains some Ladino and features well-known Turkish Sephardic performers, albeit in supporting

roles. These performers also served as consultants and Ladino coaches. According to one Ladino activist performer's exuberant exaggeration, that film did more for Ladino in two weeks than all our efforts of the past years combined!

Viewed in this context, this edition of Alfred Ascher's *Diario* is part of an exciting resurgence of interest and activity to promote Ladino. Aside from its intrinsic value, it is an important document, a primary source, a resource for students and scholars of Judeo-Spanish language, literature, culture, and history. Yet the *Diario* is different from other Ladino documents in some important respects. Like almost all contemporary creative and journalistic works in Ladino, it is written in Roman rather than Hebrew letters. Though a memoir, it reads like a fictional, picaresque adventure. Its author and central character is not (yet) a famous person, a celebrity of his time, but simply a gifted writer whose narrative, while quintessentially Sephardic, speaks to basic and essential human concerns.

The narrative begins when twenty-three-year-old Alfred and twenty-seven-year-old Albert embark on their journey. It is August 1915, and Turkey is embroiled in WWI, having entered the previous year on the side of Germany, against Russia, France, and England. The brothers intend to wait out the war in Greece, which was still neutral, and return home to Smyrna after its end, which they expect soon. But their journey is marked by unforeseen events, encounters, and decisions. They travel as planned from Smyrna to Urla, but then to three small Aegean islands: Agrio Nissi, Yatro Nissi, and, most notably, Anglo Nissi, where they spend an unexpected seven days before reaching their destination, Mytilene. From Mytilene they go on, after stopping for a day at the island of Chios, to Piraeus, the port city of Athens. This part of the journey, lasting about two weeks, is recounted in Part I, which constitutes roughly two-thirds of the *Diario*. Part II records their experiences in Piraeus and Athens, where they spend three months, and their final, unforeseen month-long voyage, beginning November 26th, from the Peloponnesian port Patras, via Algiers and Gibraltar,

to New York, where they arrive on December 25th, 1915, four and a half months after leaving Smyrna.

Though their physical journey, as outlined in this brief overview of places encountered (thirteen in all, a Jewish lucky number) and time spent in each, is interesting and impressive in itself, the real journey of the *Diario*, the meaning of their 'passages,' lies beyond time and place. Of note is that the Ladino *passajes* can mean 'passages, ways, or episodes,' and the English 'passage' can mean 'an act of passing, a transition, channel, route, crossing, lapse of time, or a piece of text or music,' and all are applicable to the *Diario*, in tune with the multiplicity that characterizes its language and views. Why else would the two weeks described in Part I take up most of the narrative? On their journey, Alfred and Albert, face many challenges and dangers as Jewish refugees, from stormy seas to hostile Greek bandits. They survive by their resourcefulness, deception, intelligence, patience, persistence, hope, humor, faith, and courage, the last of which becomes almost a leitmotif of the *Diario*, an ideal that must never be abandoned.

At least as significant as the emphasis on courage is Alfred's compassion, his feeling of kinship with other human beings that transcends all differences of religion and nationality. Like language, humanity is composed of multiple forms, each valid and connected with the others. This is the prevailing attitude of the *Diario*, in spite of the negative characterization of Turks and individual Greeks discussed above, and the mocking remarks about Christian belief. Such comments Alfred clearly addresses to his family, and entrusts to what, for all its formal presentation, he still labels a *diario*, a diary—the quintessential repository of private, perhaps fleeting and at times inappropriate thoughts and feelings. The following passage, coming as it does towards the end of the journey and narrative, says it all: ". . . to see men, women, children crying, screaming, some with the Virgin Mary, others with *tallit* and *tefillin* [Jewish prayer garment and phylacteries]—it pained me so much that I also started to cry." This magnificent image of a multiple humanity

united in prayer recalls the insightful verses of the Spanish
Hebrew poet Solomon ibn Gabirol:

> You are God.
> Your divinity and unity are inseparable,
> as is Your pre-existence and Your presence.
> It is all the same mystery.
> Though the names may be different,
> the address is the same.
>
> (*Keter Malkhut* 8:86-89, trans. Rabbi David J. Jacobs)

It is heartening, but not surprising, that this attitude of
openness and inclusiveness toward people of different religions
and cultures, which has characterized the Sephardic tradition
since the Golden Age in Muslim Spain, is exemplified in our
own time by Alfred Ascher's *Diario*.

Alfred concludes his *Diario* in typical Sephardic fashion, on
a positive note, with gratitude, hope, and touchingly expressed
devotion to family. Full of gratitude to "God and the United
States" for saving his life—life is, indeed, viewed as the prime
value in the Sephardic tradition—Alfred declares himself and
Albert "very lucky" to have found both work and women to
marry. Hoping for continued good luck, he ends with the hope
of seeing his whole family again "soon."

We don't know if Alfred's extended letter ever reached any
family members, nor even if they received the telegram that he
says he and Albert sent soon after they arrived in Mytilene; and
the fate and location of the *Diario* remain a mystery. Yet this
very mystery allows us to hope that it did, in some form, reach
some of the "dear ones" to whom it was addressed. The family
photo inscribed in French "*A mon cher fils Albert Ascher* (To my
dear son Albert Ascher)"—which appears on the page directly
following this introduction—indicates that they did in fact soon
reconnect.

In any case, the promise of Alfred's luck and his concluding hope were fulfilled to an amazing degree, and the values of the *Diario* continued to inform his and Albert's life. I remember the warm reception that fair-skinned, blue-eyed Uncle Albert, together with Aunt Matilda, gave me and my parents at their Brooklyn home. Alfred married Claire Eliscu, my beloved Auntie Claire, as planned. They settled in Far Rockaway, Queens, New York, near a fantastic beach, on the same Atlantic Ocean Alfred and Albert had crossed on their journey in 1915. After serving as head supervisor of cargo operations for several steamship companies, he retired to St. Petersburg, Florida. Alfred spent the last eight years of his life in Worcester, Massachusetts, near his daughter, Lorraine. He died on January 26th, 1986 (16 Shevat 5746).

Alfred did return to see surviving members of his family— in the summer of 1965, fifty years after his departure, and apparently, before he finished writing his *Diario*. This time he was accompanied by his younger brother Emanuel, my father, whom he invited, with typical generosity. Alfred had provided my father with his first home in this country, and much later in a time of urgent need, with a job at the steamship company. They visited their surviving sisters and brothers, not only in Smyrna, now Izmir, but also in Athens, Paris, and Israel.

My father liked to tell about their flight back to New York: when potentially dangerous turbulence was announced, Uncle Alfred reacted with a loud and enthusiastic "*Shema Israel, Adonai Eloenu, Adonai ehad!* (Hear, O Israel, the Lord our God, the Lord is One!)," the basic Jewish declaration of faith, typically exclaimed by religious Jews when facing life-threatening danger. My father found this curious and amusing because Uncle Alfred was not 'religious,' in the sense of being strictly observant; but, as indicated in the *Diario*, his Jewish identity and loyalty were unshakable. This seems to have run in the family. When I asked my usually kind and compassionate father to sign so I could spend a year in Germany on the Fulbright Grant I had been

ะwarded, he stood up tall and said, in a most menacing tone: "Don't you know what they did to us?!" This came from the ำame man who worked on the Sabbath if necessary, attended ᴐnly High Holiday services, and led a Passover seder only on (my) request. Yet his fierce identification with and loyalty to his Jewish people and tradition were, like Uncle Alfred's, unquestionable.

I remember Uncle Alfred as a suntanned, handsome, fun-loving, witty, imposing man with a sparkling smile and robust laugh. He bore a strong resemblance to my father, which both used to their mutual benefit, with typical resourcefulness and cunning. I relished the weeks my parents and I spent every summer as guests at Uncle Alfred's and Auntie Claire's home in Far Rockaway. I see my father and Uncle Alfred sporting with the waves; both were avid swimmers, as I myself became, inspired by their example. But I never heard my Uncle Alfred speak even a word of Ladino until years later, when he led a Passover seder at his daughter Lorraine's home. I was delighted to hear him intone the traditional chants and songs in our Judeo-Spanish, and to savor his justly famous Sephardic *haroset*.

I remember the generous gifts and elegant letters (in English) that Uncle Alfred sent me. I treasure his last letter, sent from St. Petersburg in 1978, probably after the death of his second wife, Beatrice Brean (Claire had died in 1949). He thanked me for my note and for my advice, which I no longer remember, but which he said gave him "courage and fortitude." Courage—how I hear this word resound now, years later, after reading his *Diario*! As Alfred Ascher continues to live in my memory, so may he, together with the values he espouses, continue to live, as a blessing and an inspiration, in the memory and actions of all who enter the world of his *Diario*!

Gloria J.Ascher
Hyannis, Massachusetts
August 2023/Elul 5783

Alfred and Albert's family in Smyrna. The French inscription in the top-left corner reads: *A mon cher fils* (to my dear son) Albert Ascher. Courtesy of David and Allen Ascher.

Souvenir de Smyrne   Golfe de Caratach

An early 20th-century postcard
featuring the Gulf of Karatash, Smyrna

DIARIO DE MI VIAJE
EN 2 PARTES
SMYRNA . TO . NEW YORK
August 10th 1915 ___ December 25th 1915

INOLVIDALVES
I
ESMOVIENTES

PASSAJES

Facsimile of the title page in the original, handwritten *Diario*

Diario de Mi Viajé

En Dos Partes
Smyrna to New York
August 10th, 1915–December 25th, 1915

Inolvidalves

i

Esmovientes

Passajes

Diary of My Journey

In Two Parts
Smyrna to New York
August 10th, 1915–December 25th, 1915

Unforgettable
and
Moving
Passages

Perfacio

La partensia que mi mano no poede escrivir ni mizmo explicarvos. Con que coraje bezi à mis queridos Ermanicos? pensando si era o no la oltima vez. La querida mama que no poude mizmo verla, todo por preservarlé sou saloud porqué si lo savia que yo iva a partir por oun tan pericolozo viajé, Dios goadré que podria aconteser, lo que no quero mizmo pensar. Ma no doudo que los quiridos Mama, papa. Ermanos. especialmente la quirida Dona Efraim i los quiridos Ermano Nissim, Ermana Behora i otros conosidos i relativos me pardonarian. No poude vervos no poudé bezarvos no poudé mizmo adressarvos oun solo biervo, i lo regretaré toda mi vida, ma todo lo izé por amor de vozotros, lo ize tambien por escapar por ouna vez por siempré de la mano de esté 'Barbaro Tourco.'

Preface

The departure that my hand cannot write nor even explain to you—what courage it took for me to kiss my dear brothers and sisters, wondering whether it would be the last time! My dear mama I could not bring myself to see, for the sake of her health, because if she had known I was going to leave for such a dangerous journey, God forbid what might have happened. I don't even want to think of it. But I do not doubt that my dear mama, papa, sisters and brothers, especially dear Dona, Efraim [Dona's husband] and dear brother Nissim, sister Behora, as well as other friends and relatives, would forgive me. I was not able to see you, I was not able to kiss you, I was not even able to say a single word to you, and I will regret it for the rest of my life, but I did everything for love of you. I also did it in order to escape once and for all from the hand of this 'Barbarous Turk.'

Parté I

Era Martes 10 Agusto por la maniana que quiti mi caza paternel en compania de mi quirido Ermano Albert por esté viajé tan estranio.

De acordo con el contrabandiero alquilimos ouna carosa que mos yevava a Ourla. Este signor mos dicho que el no podia vinir con mozotros, que no mos espantaramos que todo era mouy facil i que nada de malo mos iva a acontesser. Enfin mos entrimos en la carosa i empesimos a moestro camino. Ya pensach como mos goadrimos a no ser vistos de los caratachlis fin Cocar Yali.

Arivados aï el carossero mos izo saver que de 5 a 6 milias antes de Ourla avia ouna santinela en cada 50 passos. Le dichimos que no se espantara porqué ivamos azer todo lo possible a no ser arestados. Azevos ouna idea el danio que coriamos à oun con todo estavamos vistidos de oun coraje de fiero.

Alas 3 despoes de medio dia arivimos serca del cordon de las sentinelas. Pensi que el onico remedio era el cantar en tourco cantigas del Houriet, etc. Teniach que ver a Efraim con la fez delada fin los oigos cantando i etchando manés el coantidad que podia, el carossero mouria del espanto, la cara de Albert devino amaria. Enfin ya arivimos delantré de la primera santinela que izo quedar la carosa i queria saver ondé ivamos. Le diché en caba tourco que ivamos "Babamin Tchiflia" Selam Alekoum, i Berhaba que no manco, i oun cigaro para que no avlé mas, i ansi la escapimos de este primer pero.

Part I

It was on the morning of Tuesday, August 10th, that I left my parents' home, accompanied by my dear brother Albert, for this remarkable journey.

As agreed with the contrabandist, we hired a carriage to take us to Urla. This gentleman told us that he could not come with us, that we should not be afraid, that everything was very simple, and that nothing bad would happen to us. So we got into the carriage and started on our way. You can imagine how we kept ourselves from being seen by the people from Karatash to Cocar Yali.[1]

Upon arriving there, the driver informed us that starting from five to six miles before Urla there was a sentinel every fifty paces. We told him not to be afraid because we would do everything possible to avoid being detained. Picture to yourselves the risk we were running, even though we were clothed with a courage of iron.

At three in the afternoon we arrived near the string of sentinels. I thought that the only way out was to sing songs of the Hürriyet [political party] etc. in Turkish. You should have seen Efraim,[2] with fez cocked over his ears, singing, and rowdy drinking songs at that, as many as he could. The driver was dying of fright. Albert's face became yellow. Finally we came to the first sentinel, who stopped the carriage and wanted to know where we were going. I told him in crude Turkish that we were going to 'Babamin Chiflia,' our father's estate, said, "*Selam alekum* (Peace be upon you)," and added, "*Berhaba* (Greetings),"[3] and gave him a cigarette so he wouldn't talk any more. And so we escaped from this first dog.

1. Neighborhoods in Smyrna
2. Alfred's Hebrew name
3. Alfred implies that the addition of '*Berhaba*' is to ensure they pass as Turks

Mos adelantimos como 1 milia coando oun soldado tourco natouralmente ordeno que quedaramos. Le demandi lo que queria. Dicho que el se tenia que ir à Ourla i no tenia oun sentavo para alquilar ouna carosa, i mos rogo que lo tomaramos kon nozotros. Esto era presizamente lo que yo quiria. Naturalmenté yo le diché que ivamos al Tchiflik de noestro padre. Despoès de esto 12-15 vezes mos izieron quedar la carosa i era el signor del Soldado, que saltava diziendo que eramos los ijos de Sadik Pacha i que ivamos al Tchiflik. De esta manera arivimos a Ourla sanos i bivos. El soldado despoes de rengrasiarmos se foé para sou camino, i nozotros foimos escortados ala caza del signor contrabandiero. Era las 3 dela notché.

Despoès de esté famoso viagé ya pensach que meresiamos ouna boena comida i ouna boena cama, malorozamente no podimos obtener ni la ouna ni la otra. Foé con mouncha pena que salimos ala callé por comer coalquer coza, ma antes de salir touvimos el coudiado de mandar à mercar 2 casquetos por no ser conosidos por algouno. Comimos boeno, mos passeimos oun poco, siempré pensando, que pensavan azer con nozotros.

Retornados à caza, el signor del bandido nos izo saver que touvo preparando con oun tourco por escortarmos al famozo lugar ondé ivamos a tomar el barco para Metelin. Siempré con la falsa sounrisa en noestra cara, no tovimos que a rengrasiarlo, i dizir "All right." El reposo que touvimos esta longa notché, pensando que ivamos a confiar noestra vida a quen? A oun Tourco, no lo dezeo ni mizmo alos "Boches" "Germans."

Yo Alfred vos djouro que no dormi ni oun segondo, pensando todos mis queridos, por el viagé del procsimo dia, i pensando no ser rovado, porqué la moneda que posedavamos, la goadrava yo en mi centura, "Kimen," ma siempré armado de oun coraje de fiero i teniendo la esperansa en Dios.

We got about a mile further when, naturally, a Turkish soldier ordered us to stop. I asked him what he wanted. He said that he had to go to Urla and didn't have a cent to hire a carriage, and he asked us to take him with us. This was precisely what I wanted. Naturally, I told him we were going to our father's estate. After this they stopped the carriage twelve to fifteen times, and it was the soldier who jumped up, saying that we were the sons of Sadik Pasha and that we were going to his estate. In this way we arrived in Urla safe and sound. After thanking us, the soldier went on his way, and we were escorted to the contrabandist's house. It was eight o'clock at night.

After this glorious journey you would think that we deserved a good meal and a comfortable bed. Unfortunately, we could get neither one nor the other. With great difficulty we ventured out into the street to eat something, but before going out we took the precaution of having two caps bought for us so we would not be recognized. We ate well and took a little walk, always wondering what they were thinking of doing with us.

When we returned home, the bandit informed us that he had arranged for a Turk to escort us to the renowned place where we were going to take the boat to Mytilene. Always with a false smile on our face, we had to thank him and say *all right*.[4] The rest we had this long night, wondering how we were going to trust whom? A Turk! With our lives!—I don't wish it even to the *Germans*.

I, Alfred, swear to you that I did not sleep even a minute, thinking of all my dear ones, of the next day's journey, and thinking of how to avoid being robbed, because I kept the money we had in my special belt. But I was always armed with a courage of iron, keeping my faith in God. When it did finally dawn, it was on a day of sadness, fatigue, and fear.

4. Words originally written in English are printed in italics

Coando ya amanesio, para oun dia de tristeza, de canseria, i de miedo.

Dounqué mos levantimos, la moujer del dicho Signor nos dio oun vazo de letché a cada ouno, quon ouna galeta del tiempo de "Genovez" ma mouy savroza siendo que no teniamos que esto. Era las 7:30 coando mos izo saver que el ombré que mos iva à escortar mos queria avlar, i que mos prepararamos para salir. Despoes de ser presentados al dito signor que no era mas de oun Tourco "Gahtadji" i tenia oun "azno" con el, mos dicho que nessesavamos comer para el viajé, mos izo comprar 4 ocas de pan, quezo i zitounas.

Prontos para partir, mos dio todas las instrucciones menesterozas, mos dicho 1) tener oun corajé de bandidos, 2) mientres el viajé para tomar el barco, qualia que caminaramos siempré como 50 passos atras de el, i que al primer signal calia que mos escondieramos entré las yervas, siendo que el camino ondé ivamos a passar era por vignas. Despoes de flatarlo oun poco, como dizirlé i ivamos à ovedesser todo lo que disia siendo estavamos en sous manos, etc.

Prontos à partir el signor del Grego queria que le pagaramos antés de partir, todos mis protestos foeron en vanos, i qualia pagado. Moestro acordo era que le ivamos a pagar coando estavamos prontos para entrarmos al barco, i que todo iva a ser pagado fin Metelin. Enfin, tratimos 9 liras tourcas, demandava 10 i sous gastes que vino à Ourla, i la notché que dormimos en sou caza, todo se le pago.

Empessimos a caminar, escondiendomos cada minouto. Sin alargar sovre esté pounto, caminimos dela 8 a.m. fin las 3 p.m., coando arivimos à ouna vigna serca la mar ondé avia ouna baraca izolada. Mos asentimos, por reposar i comer, todo sin azer el mas menimo brouido, porque serca de aï avia ouna sentinela aziendo la goardia serca dela mar. El tourco mos izo saver, que alas 5, otros 6 ombres ivan à arivar al mizmo lougar, para partir con nozotros.

So we got up, and the wife of the aforementioned gentleman gave us each a glass of milk with a cookie as old as the hills, but very tasty since it was all we had. It was 7:30 when they informed us that the man who was going to escort us wanted to speak with us, and that we should prepare to leave. After we were introduced to the said gentleman, who was none other than a Turk, a lumber dealer, and had a 'jackass' with him, he told us that we needed food for the journey. He made us buy four pounds of bread, cheese, and olives.

When we were ready to leave, he gave us all the necessary instructions. He told us, 1) to have the courage of bandits, and 2) that during the trip on the way to the boat we should always walk about fifty paces behind him, and that at the first signal we should hide in the grasses, since the path we were taking went through vineyards. We flattered him a little, telling him that we would obey him in everything he said, since we were in his hands, etc.

When we were about to leave, the Greek gentleman wanted us to pay him before leaving. All my protests were in vain, and I had to pay him. Our agreement had been that we would pay him when we were ready to get on the ship, and that everything would be paid for up to Mytilene. So we offered 9 Turkish liras. He asked for 10, plus his expenses for his trip to Urla and for the night that we slept at his house. He was paid for everything.

We started to walk, hiding every minute. To make a long story short, we walked from 8 a.m. until 3 p.m., when we arrived at a vineyard near the sea, where there was an isolated shed. We sat down to rest and eat, without making the slightest noise, because nearby, near the sea, a sentinel was standing guard. The Turk informed us that at five o'clock another six men were going to arrive at the same place to depart with us. I asked him if he knew where the ship was. He knew nothing and said that another man was already preparing everything.

Le demandi si savia onde estava el barco, i no savia nada, diziendo que otro ombré ya estava preparando todo.

Sigoun dicho alas 5:30 los ombrés que esperavamos vigneron. Todos eran gregos, bandidos de la mas bacha classa, i el onico remedio era fraternizarmos con eyos, lo que izimos. Media ora mas tadré el ombré ditcho, que preparava todo, arivo, diziendo que calia que estouvieramos en el mizmo lougar fin que retornava el, i partio el otro tourco que mos escorto aï i esté partio, i quedimos solos, quero dizir 8 personas, sin saver que se iva azer. Ya vos imajinach el miedo, i pensando no sea que era un djogo que mos djugaron i estavamos en el lougar el mas daniozo, no poder avlar no poder foumar, escouro.

Enfin, despoes de tanta agonia el ombré retorno, diziendo que mos prepararamos para otro viagé, asigourandomos que no avia el mas menimo espanto, si sigueamos sous instrucciones, que era caminar con el mas grande reposo i acavido. Mos dicho que el foé al posto militar serca de aï, que se composia de oun bach Tchaouch i dos soldados i con protesto que era Corban—Baïram aquea notché, los invito à sou Tschiflic para comer, i esto era ouna prova de mas como no avia espanto.

Dounqué empessimos à caminar de las 8:30 fin las 11:30 i arivimos serca de la mar. Ai mos dicho que no calia que izieramos el mas menimo rouido, ni que foumaran, porqué mouy serca de aï se topava otro posto. Despoes de repozarmos oun poco, mos ordeno de quitar los calsados i los tchourapés porqué calia caminar en la mar 5 o 10 minoutos. Como ya tomimos el mal a passensia i siempré pensando que era mijor adelantar que de ir atras, lo izimos, i como mo lo fadaron, empessimos à caminar, la agua fin los dizes, i pizando en la arena, mesclada con piedresicas, que pintcharon mas que vidros. Oh! esto no se comia, los otros 6 no se quechavan

As he said, at 5:30 the men we were waiting for came. They were all Greeks, bandits of the lowest class, and the only way out for us was to fraternize with them, which we did. Half an hour later the aforementioned man who was preparing everything arrived, saying that we had to stay in that same place until he returned. The other Turk, who had escorted us there, left, and this one left, and we were left alone—eight people, without knowing what was going to happen. You can imagine our fear as we prayed: let it not be a trick that they played on us! We were in the most deplorable situation—we couldn't speak, we couldn't smoke . . . dark.

Finally, after such a stressful time, the man returned, saying that we should prepare for another trip, assuring us that we had not the slightest reason to fear if we followed his instructions, which were: walk with utmost calm and caution. He told us that he had gone to the military post near there, that it consisted of one sergeant major and two soldiers, and that, on the pretext that that night was a Day of Sacrifice, he had invited them to eat at his estate—this was one more reason not to be afraid.

And so we started to walk. We walked from 8:30 till 11:30, when we arrived near the sea. There he told us that we must not make the slightest noise, nor smoke, because very close by there was another post. After we had rested a little, he ordered us to take off our shoes and socks because we had to walk in the sea for five or ten minutes. Since we accepted the bad situation with patience, always thinking it was better to go forward than back, we did it, and since this was the fate allotted to us, we began to walk, with the water up to our knees. Stepping on the sand mixed with tiny stones that pierced sharper than glass—oh, that was hard to take! The other six did not complain because they were used to walking barefoot. In a word, it was worse than Hell.

porqué ya estavan ouzados à caminar descalso, en pocos tiervos era mas negro que el Enfirno.

Caminimos ansi fin ke arivimos à oun piniasco, yo i Albert estavamos coajé entezados, mos vistimos, i el ombré mos izo saver que calia esperar como 2 oras fin que ouna barca iva a vinir para yevarmos à ouna tchica isla azolada ondé ivamos à tomar el barco. Enfin! despoes de 2 o 3 oras de agonia, vimos vinir ouna barquita, se aserco, i sin avlar ni oun solo biervo, nos descalsimos de nuevo, para entrarmos. Despoes de entrarmos mos dicheron que mos echaramos largos, i moudos.

Despoes de navigar como 3 coartos de ora arivimos à ouna izla, apenas desbarquimos, despoes de tomar las instructiones menesterozas que la barca se alecho, i con la prissa que salimos mos olvidimos el pan i todo en la barca de manera que quedimos sin nada que comer.

Agora vos vo a explicar las ditchas instruccionés. Esta isla se nombra Agrio Nissi, es jousto enfrente de Ourla, de la ouna parté de la isla se ve Ourla i de la otra parté se ve otra isla de nombre Yatro Nissi. Dounqué los ombrés que mos decharon aï mos dicheron de irmos devista de la otra parte de la isla, i de etchar flamadas. Eran signal para otros contrabandieros, en Yatro Nissi. Estos signores estavan de acordo quon estos que coando vian foego vinian, i tomavan alos que avia para embarcarlos para Metelin.

Ya savech que avia 6 gregos con nozotros, ouno mas torpé de otro. Estos signores querian azer el foego de la parte de Ourla. Ya creech que era yamar alos tourcos i que izieron lo que querian. Ya vos imaginach la pena i los pletos que touvé con estos torpés a darles a entender el pericolo que coriamos. Despoes de tantas penas ya entendieron, i me nominaron sous capitan, i quedimos de acordo que todo lo que les dezia yo ivan azer.

We walked like this until we came to a large rock. Albert and I were almost frozen. We got dressed, and the man informed us that we had to wait two more hours until a boat would come to take us to a small, isolated island, where we were going to take the ship. Finally, after two or three more stressful hours, we saw a little boat coming. It approached, and without even saying a word we took off our shoes and socks again to get on board. After we had gotten on board they told us to lie down flat and remain silent.

After traveling for about three quarters of an hour, we arrived at an island. Right away we disembarked, after receiving the necessary instructions. The boat departed. We had left in such a hurry that we forgot the bread and everything on the boat, so we were left with nothing to eat.

Now I will tell you about the instructions. This island, called Agrio Nissi (Wild Island), is right in front of Urla. From one side of the island you can see Urla, and from the other side you can see another island, called Yatro Nissi (Physician Island). The men who left us there told us to go right away to the other side of the island and throw flame signals, which would be signals to the other contrabandists in Yatro Nissi. These gentlemen had agreed that when they saw the fire they would come and pick up those who were there to transport them to Mytilene.

As you know, there were six Greeks with us, one more stupid than the other. These gentlemen wanted to make the fire on the Urla side, would you believe it, which would be like summoning the Turks to do what they wanted! You can imagine the trouble and the arguments I had with those dumbbells to make them understand the danger we were risking. After so much trouble, they did understand, and they nominated me their captain, and we agreed that they would do everything I told them.

Mos foïmos de la otra parte de la isla i ordeni que
etcharan foego, en mizmo tiempo espantandomos porque
los projectorés del castillo, quero dizir del porto de Smyrna,
caillan djousto onde estavamos. No avia otro remedio, qualia
etchado flamadas, i esto foe lo que izimos por media ora, i
ningouno vinia. Ala fin les diché que se repozaran fin al
amaneser, i esto foé lo que todos izimos.

Cuando amanesió ya se vido la otra isla en ouna bien longa
lechoura, ma ningouno no vinia ni se via nada aï. Empessimos
a azer signales con rizas, otro con ouna savana blanca, ma todo
en vano, siendo que no se via nada. Pensad el desespero de mi
i de Albert, ma siempre sin pedrer corajé. Dounqué alas 8:30
vimos à ouna mouy longa distansia ouna barquita a vela, que
vinia a noestra direction. Aqui el espanto fue mas mountcho
que siempre, siendo que no saviamos si eran los tourcos o los
otros, porque yo pensava que la resplandor de los foegos que
etchimos la notché podia ser que vieron de Ourla, i vinian
para insepectar el logar. Ma a mezura que se asercavan ya se
podia ver que no eran Militares, dé manera que ya touvimos
oun poco mas de corajé.

Enfin la famoza barca se aserco i gritaron en grego coalo
queriamos, i antes que avlaran el sigoundo biervo ya les
dichimos todo, i mos tomaron con eyos, para yevarmos a
Yatro Nissi. Apenas mos alechimos 50 metros de la isla, mos
dicheron que calia que pagaramos 40 Francos por persona
para ser transportados à esta isla. Todas las protestasionés
foé en vano, mos condenavan de retournarmos ala isla
si no pagavamos lo que demandavan. Eran 4 Bandidos i
armados, de revolveres, i fusiles, no avia remedio, calia pagar.
Yo les diché que les iva a pagar coando arivavamos ala isla,
i la razon era, que la moneda la goadrava en el "quimer"
"Centoura" i no queria mostrarles que tenia mas plata, ma
esto los raviava, i querian los 80 Francos imediatamenté.

We went to the other side of the island, and I ordered them to throw flame signals, though I was, at the same time, afraid, because projectiles from the fortress, that is, the port of Smyrna, would fall exactly where we were. There was no other option—we had to throw flame signals, and that is what we did for half an hour. Nobody came. Finally, I told them to rest until dawn, and that's what we all did.

When dawn came, we could see the other island very far away, but nobody came, nor did we see anything there. We started to make signals with handkerchiefs—one used a white bed sheet, but all in vain, since nothing could be seen. Imagine the despair Albert and I felt, but always without losing courage. Then at 8:30 we saw, in the far distance, a little boat under sail that was coming in our direction. Now the fear was greater than before, because we didn't know if they were the Turks or the others. I thought they might have seen from Urla the brilliance of the fire signals that we had thrown during the night, and they were coming to inspect the place. But as they came closer, we could see that they were not military, so we had a little more courage.

Finally, the renowned boat approached, and they cried out in Greek, asking what we wanted. Before they could say another word, we told them everything, and they took us with them to transport us to Yatro Nissi. As soon as we were fifty meters away from the island, they told us that we had to pay 40 francs per person to be transported to this island. All protestations were in vain. They threatened to take us back to the island if we didn't pay what they asked. They were four bandits armed with revolvers and rifles. There was no other way—we had to pay. I told them I would pay when we arrived at the island, the reason being that I kept the money in a special belt and didn't want to show them that I had more.

Con mouncha pena i en metiendo Albert delantré de mi ya poudé quitar lo que demandavan, i les pagui.

Enfin ya arivimos à esta binditcha Yatro Nissi. Ala salida encontrimos otra troupa de bandidos gregos ourlalis. Ouno de entre eyos vistido de Soldado grego Yeritli, natouralmente armado, se aserco de nozotros i mos demando lo que eramos, de ondé veniamos, onde ivamos i otras mil questiones. Entré todos las repoestas la mijor que le gousto foe coando le diché que eramos Francezes.

Mos encorajo que no teniamos miedo, que el mizmo era plaçado aï por las otoridades Francezas i Englesas para ver lo que se passava en estas agoas que eran tourcas, i que el estava siempré en comonicacion con las Marinas Aliadas i mos dicho, que aquel dia mizmo mos ivamos en oun Barco grande i mos iva a yevar a otra isla, Anglo Nissi, English Adassi, i que aï se topava siempré ounos coantos tourpilliorés Aliados. Dounqué esto estava mouy boeno. Esto foé todo lo que mos dicho.

Caminimos oun poco por aqui i aï i embezimos que aï se topavan 106 gregos fouidos de la Armada Tourca que se ivan a embarcar con mozotros para Metelin. Yo pensi que era boena idea familiarizarmos con eyos i que en aziendo ansi poede ser que mos davan coal quer coza para comer porqué nozotros sigoun ya vos escrivi mos olvidimos lo que teniamos en la barca.

Well, la primera reception foé con "Ovreï" "Bohorakeys" "Tchifouités" i otros boenos biervos fin que les izé entender que eramos Francezes i que calia que mos trataran boeno, que si no, iva a reportar todo al Comandanté Franses de la otra isla, ondé esperavamos partir de oun minouto al otro. Esto foé ouna boena milizina para estos Bandidos, devista todos devinieron amigos, i dandomoz todo lo que tenian, i esto es lo que queria el tchilibi de Efraïm.

But that made them angry, and they wanted the 80 francs right away. By placing Albert in front of me I was able, with a lot of effort, to take out what they asked, and I paid them.

Finally, we arrived at this blessed Yatro Nissi. Upon disembarking, we encountered another troop of Greek bandits from Urla. One of them, who was dressed like a Greek soldier, and, naturally, armed, approached us and asked us what we were, where we came from, where we were going, and a thousand other questions. Of all the answers, the one he liked best was when I told him that we were Frenchmen.

He urged us not to be afraid and said that he himself was placed there by the French and English authorities to see what was happening in these waters, which were Turkish, and that he was in constant communication with the Allied navies. He also told us that on that very day we were going on a large boat, and that he would take us to another island, Anglo Nissi, English Adassi, and that at that island there were always some Allied torpedo boats, so this was very good. This was all he told us.

We walked a little this way and that, and we learned that there were 106 Greek refugees from the Turkish army who were going to embark with us for Mytilene. I thought it was a good idea to make friends with them—maybe they would give us something to eat, because, as I wrote you, we forgot what we had taken along on the boat.

Well, the first *reception* we got was "*Uvrei, Bohorakeys, Chifuites* [derogatory terms for Jews]" and other good words, until I made them understand that we were Frenchmen, and that they had to treat us well. If not, I was going to report everything to the French Commandant of the other island, for which we hoped to leave any minute. That was good medicine for those bandits. Right away they all became our friends, giving us all they had—and that is what the gentleman[5] Efraim wanted.

---

5. *Tchilibi,* transliterated from Turkish: "a well-bred, educated gentleman"

Ouna ora mas tadre todos mos embarquimos en el grande barco que avia stationado aï para irmos ala otra isla que se yama Inglis adasi. Despoes de navigar mas de 3 oras arivimos a esta isla, ma no encontrimos nada que solo cazas vazias. Esta isla era poevlada de gregos i foeron algounos matados i otros expulsados por los tourcos. Salimos aï, i el capo mos disho que calia repozarmos por 1 o 2 oras, i que mas tadré ivamos a caminar de la otra parté de la isla, onde ivamos à encontrar la basa naval Aliada.

Por oun minouto me recoerdo las chenas estranjeras que encontrimos en esta isla, las casas midias derocadas o quemadas, la furnitoura (el moblé) todo en pedasos, pedasos de ropa i de lingerie embatacados de sangré, cavéos de moujeres a massos, en todos los cantonés, en oun biervo era horriblé al ver esto todo, todo etcho por los Tourcos.

Enfin, alas 5 p.m. empessimos a caminar. Vos imajinach 108 ombrés formava ouna boena Armada. Despoes de caminar fin las 8:30 arivimos de la otra parté de la isla, ondé passimos la notché en ouna Iglesia deziertada, pensando que ala maniana porcsima mos ivamos a embarcar en algoun vapor Frances o Ingles. La notché se passo mouy boena, dormimos porqué estavamos mouy fatigados.

Ala maniana, a moestro grande encanto, mos vimos nada, ni Franceses ni vaporos. Foï, le demandi al capo que se iva azer. Mos dicho que no mos dezesperaramos, i que cuando el sol se iva a levanter tenia oun remedio para azer atirar la attencion de los vapores mizmo si estavan a ouna distensia de 200 milias, i el remedio era, que el se iva a souvir à ouna montagna alta que avia aï i con la ayouda de oun espejo, mirando el Sol, las solombras iva atirar sous attencion. El signor se foé aï ariva i estouvo coajé todo el dia sin ningoun resoultado. Ala notché, ensendio ouna lanterna i se foé a el mizmo lougar, ma siempré lo mizmo, porque nada no aparesia.

An hour later we all embarked on the large boat that was stationed there to go to the other island, which is called Inglis Adasi. After traveling more than three hours, we arrived at this island, but we encountered nothing, only empty houses. This island used to be inhabited by Greeks, some of whom had been killed and others expelled by the Turks. We disembarked there, and the leader told us that we had to rest one or two hours, for later we were going to walk on the other side of the island, where we would arrive at the Allied naval base.

For a moment I recall the strange scenes we encountered on this island: the houses half destroyed or burned, the furniture all in pieces, pieces of clothing and of lingerie stained with blood, clumps of women's hair in every corner. In a word, it was horrible to see all of this, all done by the Turks.

At 5 p.m. we started to walk. You can imagine what a fine army these 108 men made! After walking until 8:30 we arrived at the other part of the island, where we spent the night in a deserted church, expecting that the next morning we would board some French or English ship. The night passed very well. We slept, as we were very tired.

In the morning, to our great amazement, we saw nothing, neither Frenchmen nor ships. I went and asked the leader what was going to happen. He told us not to despair, for come sunrise, he had a plan to attract the attention of ships, even if they were 200 miles away. The plan was that he would climb one of the high mountains in the area, and, with the aid of a mirror facing the sun, the shadows would attract their attention. The man went up there and stayed almost the whole day, but with no results. At night he lit a lantern and went to the same place, but the situation remained the same—nothing appeared.

Meanwhile, on that day we sustained ourselves with grapes and figs that were there, more than enough. You can understand that, since we expected to arrive in Mytilene in

En mientré aquel mizmo dia mos mantouvimos con ouva i igos, que avia aï mas que bastanté. Ya pensach que cada ouno de nozotros, pensando que ivamos à arivar a Metelin en oun dia, no mos reservimos nada de comer. Nozotros no se quere citcho no teniamos absolutamente nada, i foe grasias a estos Gregos que poedimos obtener algo—ma ouva i igos a sovrar. Passimos el primer dia, i se tomo el mal a passensia.

El segoundo dia foe lo mizmo que el primero, por mas peor de esta parté de la isla no avia cazas, era todo vignas, de manera que calia estar en el Sol el dia entero, i la notché dormir en lo avierto. El dia entero caminando, dourmiendo i comiendo ouva i igos, grassias a esto como no ivamos a morir de ambré. Dounque sigoun se passo el sigoundo dia, ansi foé el tresero, el coarteno, el sinqueno, el seteno. Por siete dias, no bevimos agoa. No quero mountcho alargar en esté sojeto, porqué es mouy tristé. Vozotros creo que ya vos azesh ouna idea como se passaron estos 7 dias.

Al seten dia por la tadré, mos reounimos todos i con el Capo decidimos a mandar 2 o 3 ombres dela otra parté dela izla, a que izieron traer el tchournié que mos troucho de Yatro Nissi a Ingless Adassi, i el escopo era que ivamos a esperar fin el procsimo dia, i que ningoun vapor no se asercava de la izla, moz ivamos a entrar todos al tchournie i ivamos à partir para onde mos yevava el ayré. Dounqué era 4 p.m. coando mandimos 2 gregos para azer traer el barco.

Alas 5:30 p.m. vimos a ouna sierta lechoura por la primera vez en 7 dias fumo de vapor. Ya vos imajinach como todos, empessimos a azer signales con rizas i con todo lo que poudiamos para azer atirar la atention del vapor—à moestra boena furtuna el vapor se empesso à asercar, i vino a ouna distensia ondé podiamos ver que era oun torpillior Ingless.

Enfin vino serca dela izla, i izieron abachar ouna barca, con 5 ombres vinieron a tierra, i empessaron a enterogarmos quen eramos, i de ondé veniamos, por todo, i con la ayuda de

one day, not one of us kept anything to eat. We shouldn't say that we had absolutely nothing; thanks to those Greeks we could get something, and grapes and figs we even had left over. We got through the first day, accepting the bad situation with patience.

The second day was the same as the first, only worse, for on this part of the island there were no houses, it was all vineyards. We had to stay out in the sun all day long and sleep in the open air at night. The whole day walking, sleeping and eating grapes and figs—thanks to that we wouldn't die of hunger. Thus the second day passed, and so went the third, the fourth, the fifth, the sixth, and the seventh. For seven days we drank no water. I don't want to dwell too much on this subject because it's very sad. I think you have some idea of how we spent those seven days.

On the afternoon of the seventh day, we all met together and, with the leader, decided to send two or three men to the other part of the island, where they had brought the fishing boat that transported us from Yatro Nissi to Ingles Adassi. The plan was to wait until the next day, and if no ship approached the island, all of us would board the fishing boat and set out for wherever the wind would take us. It was 4 p.m. when we sent two Greeks out to bring the boat.

At 5:30 p.m. we saw in the distance, for the first time in seven days, the steam from a ship. You can imagine how we all started to make signals with handkerchiefs and everything we could to attract the attention of the ship. It was our good fortune that the ship began to approach. It came close enough for us to see that it was an English torpedo boat.

Finally, it came close to the island and let down a boat with five men, who came on land. They began to interrogate us, asking who we were, where we were from—about everything; and, with the help of an interpreter, a Greek they had with them, we told them, first of all, that we were dying of hunger,

oun entrepreta, grego que tenian con eyos, antes de todo les dichimos que mouriamos de ambré, i que queriamos partir onde foessé, pourvu, que salieramos de aï. El Oficier mos dicho que iva ir a reportar todo al Capitan, i iva a retornar con repoesta.

Foe a bordo, i despoes de 10-15 minoutos torno con la barca yena de comania, i raporto que el capitan no mos podia tomar sin tener orden del Amiral i que malorozamente era mouy tadré a comonicar por el telegrafo sin ilo. I mos dicho agora comé boeno, i no vos desesperech, nozotros vamos azer todo lo possible a retornar, maniana por la maniana, i vos vamos a transportar, onde dize el Amiral. I yo no manqui de dizirle, ke eramos Franceses, i mos dicho que iva a raportarlo tambien al Amiral Franças, i despoes de retornar a bordo partieron devista.

Agora vos dire oun poco en lo que la comania consestia. 1) 10 cachas de Biscuit a 25 Kilos la cacha, 2) 5 cachas de carne de vaca en coutis, bien preparada i delicioza, i cada cacha contenia 5 coutis de tenekié à 5 Kilos el couti 3) 2 cachicas de quezo, 4) 10 coutis de frouta preservada, 5) 150 coutis de tenekié contieniendo 100 cigarros en cada couti, (i espritos), ounas coantas pipas con Tobacco, 6) 15 couvas de agoa con bouz, i en troco de esto todo, les dimos 2 sestos de igos frescos con ouva que teniamos siempré en reserve. Ya vos imaginach la alegria de todos coando empessimos a comer i bever, la primera vez en 7 dias, i comimos, comimos, comimos fin que mos . . . artimos.

Agora veremos a lo que se izo de los 2 ombres que mandimos de la otra parte de la izla, para azer traer el tchournie. Estos dos ombres partieron alas 4 p.m. i los esperavamos alas 8. Dounqué las 8 sono, despoes las 9, 10, 11—i los ombres no venian, i todos empesimos a pensar a lo que devino de ellios.

and that we wanted to depart for wherever, just as long as we could get out of here. The officer said he would report everything to the captain and return with the answer.

He went on board, and after 10-15 minutes he returned with the boat filled with provisions. He reported that the captain could not take us without having orders from the admiral, and that it was, unfortunately, too late to communicate by wireless telegraph. So he told us: "For now, eat well, and don't despair! We are going to do everything possible to return tomorrow morning, and we will transport you to where the admiral says." I didn't miss the chance to tell him that we were Frenchmen, and he promised to report this to the French admiral. They departed immediately after returning on board.

Now I'll tell you a little about what was in the provisions: 1) 10 crates of crackers, 25 kilos a crate 2) 5 crates of canned beef, nicely prepared and delicious - each crate contained 5 tin cans, 5 kilos a can 3) two little crates of cheese 4) 10 cans of preserved fruit 5) 150 tin cans with 100 cigarettes in each can (with matches) and some pipes of *tobacco* 6) 15 barrels of water with ice. In exchange for all this, we gave him two baskets of fresh figs with grapes, which we always had in reserve. You can imagine the pleasure we all felt when we began to eat and drink, for the first time in seven days! We ate and ate and ate, until we . . . were full.

Now let's see what happened to the two men we sent to the other part of the island to bring the boat. These two men had left at 4 p.m., and we expected them back at 8. Eight o'clock came, then 9, 10, 11, and the men didn't come. We all started to wonder what had become of them.

I should tell you that this Ingles Adassi is located precisely vis-à-vis Karaburun, and we all knew that the Turks had military observation points there. Some said that the boat had been captured by the Turks, and that the Turks had surely

Antes de nada vos diré, que esta Ingless Adassi es situada cjousto vis-à-vis de Cara Bournou, i todos saviamos que los tourcos tenian aï pountos de Observation militar. Ounos cizian, que el tchournie foe capturado por los tourcos, i que los tourcos sigouramente vieron el torpillior Ingless ancorar serca de Ingless Adassi. Cada ouno i ouno dizia ouna coza, i el espanto era general, porque como nada los tourcos podian ᵔinir aï, i Dios savia lo ke ivamos a devenir.

El capo ordeno que no foumaran i que los que possedavan arma como revolver o cotchio, que levantaran la mano, i entre 106 ombres avia 40 à 50 que tenian armas. I les dicho, si se podian defender i protectar à los otros, en cavzo que los tourcos vinian. Despoes que todos acceptaron, los plasso, à 5 i a 10, en prontos, que el savia mijor, para observar, i que el momento que vian algo, de chouflar, i los otros ivan a venir a sous ayouda. Esto ditcho, los yamo a estos que tenían armas i las plaso, ounos serca la mar, a otros en el tépé (mountagna). I los otros todos sin avlar, sin foumar estouvimos arecojidos en oun lougar. Moestras amunitiones consestian de 10 fusiles 25 revolveres, i coutchios.

I todos estouvieron sigoun el orden de capo fin las 2 dela maniana coando sobito, sintimos gritos, que venian de lechos en la mar. Todos acostavan las orejas para sintir lo que se passava, sin poder responder ni mizmo avlar oun biervo. Enfin mas tadré, sintimos bien claro, que los que gritavan eran los 2 ombres que mandimos i que querian que izieramos oun foego (flamada) para que vieran ondé ivan à ancorar el barco siendo que todo por aï era piniasco. Dounqué, izimos el foego sin piedrer tiempo, i el barco se aserco, los 2 ombres vinieron a tierra, i mos dicheron que se piedreron i no savian onde ancorar.

Despoes todos mos arecojimos de noevo, i durmimos fin la maniana. Ala maniana esperimos por el retorno del torpilior o por otro vapor. Ya era las 9, 10, i no viamos vinir nada.

seen the English torpedo boat anchored near Ingles Adassi. Everyone said something, and we were all afraid that the Turks could easily come here. Only God knew what would become of us.

The leader ordered us not to smoke and asked those who possessed a weapon such as a revolver or a knife to raise their hand. Among the 106 men there were 40 to 50 who had arms. He asked them if they could defend and protect the others in case the Turks came, and, after they had all agreed, he positioned them, five or ten at each observation point, which he knew better than the others. The minute they saw anything they were to whistle, and the others would come to their aid. That said, he called those who had arms and positioned them, some near the sea, others on the mountain. The rest of us, without speaking, without smoking, were gathered together in one place. Our weapons consisted of 10 rifles, 25 revolvers, and knives.

All remained stationed as the leader had ordered until 2 in the morning, when suddenly we heard screams coming from far away, in the sea. All strained their ears to hear what was happening, without being able to respond or even to utter a word. Finally, we heard very clearly and realized that those who were screaming were the two men we had sent. They wanted us to throw a flame signal so they could see where to anchor the boat, for the terrain there consisted exclusively of large rocks. So we made the fire without losing any time, and the boat approached. The two men came on land and told us that they had gotten lost and didn't know where to lay anchor.

Then we all gathered together again and slept until the morning. That morning we were hoping for the return of the torpedo boat or for another ship. It was 9 o'clock, 10, and we saw nothing coming. Without a moment to lose, we, except for 30 men, decided to leave in the rotted boat. We got into the boat, and it was so weighed down that there was a hand's

San piedrer tiempo, ala exseption de 30 ombres, decidimos de partir con el barco poudrido, i mos entrimos al barco, i estava tan cargado, fin que avia oun palmo de la agoa al tchournié. Ayré no avia, de manera, que se nessesitava remar. Ya vos i imaginach, que a poder de remar lo que se podia realizar era 1/2 milia a la ora. Grasias a Dios depoes de ouna ora, touvimos cun poco de airé, alevantimos las velas, i ya se poudo realizar oun poco mas de prestés. Ma el barco era tan poudrido, que empesso a entrar agoa, todos siempré con un coraje de fiero, sin avlar sin menar, de miedo que no se aboltara el barco.

Enfin coando arivimos a ouna lechoura de 25-30 milias, vimos oun vapor que vinia a moestra direction, ma era tan lechos que no se conosia que nationalidad era. Coando se aserco oun poco mas, vimos que era Françes, i a mizoura que se asercava, viamos que el vapor signalava con vilicas, de mil colores, ma quen entendia lo que querian. Ma el capitan del barco dicho que etsas vilicas singnifican, que el barco se entregara, i para azerles saver, que estavamos a sous disposition, izimos abachar moestras velas.

Enfin el vapor se aserco de nozotros, en mientres yo les diché a todos los gregos, que coando el vapor se aserca, que empessen a gritar "Vive la France!" Ya vos imaginach el brouïdo de 108 personas gritando en medio de mar "Vive la France!" A mizoura que gritavamos, el equipatchio del vapor ivan aplodiendo. Enfin el vapor se quedo— El vapor se yamava "La Rochelle Ginette" (Saint Nazaire), i mos etcharon ouna coedra, i acostimos el barco, i aquea ora el tchilibi de Efraïm salio gritando "Nous sommes de Français, Monsieur le Capitain, ayez pitié de nous, nous mourons de faim!"

I el Capitan, oun djoveno, abacho del Ponte, i me demando coantos Franceses avia a bordo, i le diché que avia solo 2 Ermanos, i mos yamo que souvieramos a bordo, mos quitimos los cachetos, mos apreto la mano, i mos yevo à sou cabina, i le conti todo lo que ya savech i oun poco mas,

breadth of water on the bottom. There was no wind, so we had to row. You can imagine that by rowing we could only make half a mile an hour. Thank God, after an hour there was a little wind. We put up the sails, and we could gain a little speed, but the boat was so rotted that water began to come in. All remained as ever with a courage of iron, without talking, without moving, afraid that the boat would overturn.

Finally, when we had traveled the distance of 25-30 miles, we saw a ship coming in our direction, but it was so far away that we couldn't tell what nationality it was. When it came a little closer, we saw that it was French, and when it came closer still, we saw that the ship was signaling with little flags of a thousand colors—but who understood what they wanted? The captain of the boat said that these little flags signified that our boat should surrender. To let them know that we were at their disposal, we lowered our sails.

Finally, as the ship was approaching us, I told all the Greeks that when it came real close they should start shouting "*Vive la France!*" (Long live France!). You can imagine the sound of 108 people in the middle of the sea shouting "*Vive la France!*" As long as we kept on shouting, the crew of the ship kept on applauding. Then the ship, La Rochelle Ginette (Saint Nazaire), stood still, and they threw us a rope, and we came closer to the ship. At that moment the gentleman Efraim came out, shouting, "*Nous sommes de Français! Monsieur le Capitaine, ayez pitié de nous, nous mourrons de faim!*" (We are Frenchmen! Captain, sir, have pity on us, we're dying of hunger!)

The captain, a young man, came down from the bridge and asked me how many Frenchmen were on board. I told him there were only two brothers, and he asked us to come on board. We took off our caps, and he shook our hands and brought us to his cabin. I told him everything you already know and a little more. He asked us if we had had lunch

_ mos demando si ya aviamos almorzado, ha, ha, ha, i yamo al couzindero i les dicho que mos diera algo que comer, mientrés que los gregos en el barco gritavan siempré "Vive la France!"

Comimos boeno, i souvi a ver al Capitan por demandarle que iva azer kon mozotros, i con los otros del barco, i los otros que quedaron en la izla, i mos dicho, à vozotros 2 vos vo a tener aqui a bordo fin que arivamos a algoun porto, i el barco con los ombres adientro lo va atar detras del vapor, i los va a travar, mientrés que por los otros en la isla no podia azer nada. I foé que despoes de tantas rogativas, tomo a todos a bordo, i les dio caffé i pan, i quezo, ato el barco vazio al vapor, i empesso a irsé para la direction dela isla.

Todo foe boeno por ounos coantos minoutos, coando que el vapor se quedo, i el Capitan me izo saver que estava en comonication con oun torpillior Ingless en la isla i que el torpillior tenia a bordo los 30 ombres que quedaron aï, i que venia a encontrar a moestro vapor para tomarmos a todos a bordo i yevarmos a Metelin. Dounque el vapor espero como 1 ora i el Torpillior vino, se aserco del vapor, i mos tomo a todos, i el Capitan Frances le dicho al Capitan del torpillior, que mos diera "Special Attention" siendo que eramos Franceses. Dounque de aï a Metelin touvimos un viagé fino, el torpillior azia 25 millias por ora.

Arivados à Metelin alas 10:30 p.m., i empessimos a debarcar en los barcos que vinieron del porto, coando todos los barcos arivaron al passaporto no los decharon salir a tierra, diziendo que en Metelin no avia lougar para resfouïdos, i que calia que se embarcaran para Pereo, en oun vapor que iva a partir devista. Yo i Albert decidimos de desbarcar aï costa que costa, porque estavamos mouy fatigados, i no teniamos foersas para suportar otro viajé sin reposarmos alo menos oun dia, i demandimos que queriamos avlar al Oficier en cargo del passaporto, Enfin lo vimos i le mostrimos moestros papeles como eramos Francesses. Despoes que mos izo

(*hahaha!*), and summoned the cook and told him to give us something to eat, while the Greeks in the boat continued to shout "*Vive la France!*"

We ate well. I went up to see the captain to ask him what he was going to do with us and with the others on the boat and with those who had stayed on the island. He told us, "You two I'm going to keep here on board until we reach a port." The boat with the men inside he was going to tie up in back of the ship and pull, but he could do nothing for the others on the island. It turned out that, after so much pleading, he took everyone on board, gave them coffee and bread and cheese, tied the empty boat to the ship, and set out in the direction of the island.

Everything went well for a few minutes. Then the ship stood still. The captain informed me that they were in contact with an English torpedo boat at the island, and that the torpedo boat had on board the 30 men who had remained there. It was coming to meet our ship in order to take us on board and bring us to Mytilene. The ship waited for about an hour, and the torpedo boat came, approached the ship, and took us all on board. The French captain told the captain of the torpedo boat to give us *special attention* because we were French. So from there to Mytilene we had a good trip. The torpedo boat traveled 25 miles an hour.

We arrived at Mytilene at 10:30 p.m. and began to disembark into the boats that came from the port—when all boats that were arriving at the port of call were not allowed to land. They said that in Mytilene there was no room for refugees. They would have to set out for Piraeus in a ship that was going to depart soon. Albert and I decided to disembark there, whatever the consequences, because we were very tired and didn't have the strength to endure another voyage without resting for at least one day. We asked to speak to the officer in charge. Finally, we got to see him and showed him our papers

e perar algouna media ora, mos dicho que ya podiamos debarcar.

Ouna vez en tiera, mos foimos al Berber porqué ya mos avia cressido "Chehina" i despoes mos foimos al Hotel, onde courmimos fin la 11 dela maniana. Caminimos oun poco, i vos telegrafimos devista de muestro arivo.

La primera coza que me occupi foe de bouchcar onde era el Consolato Français i tcharpearlé ounas coantas "hatahots". Dounque ya lo topimos, le di a entender moestros dertes (Era grego, no avlava mizmo el Français). Enfin, despoes de rompermé la cavesa con el por tomarlé algo, mos dizia siempré que el no tenia la otorita a gastar ni oun centavo por el governo Français, de manera que no mos podia ayoudar. Ma despoes de enfastiarlo mountchas vezes, mos dicho que para escaparla de mi, estava pronto, a darmos ouna letra para la Compania de Vapores para Pereo aque mos diera oun passaje gratis para Pereo, 2⁰ classa i que dinero era empossiblé a darmos, i mos dio ouna letra de recomandation para ouna Societa de Bienfesensia en Metelin i que probablementé mos ayoudarian.

Que, piedré oun minouto? Foïmos aï, mostrimos la letra, i la remetieron ala persona que era adressada, mozotros esperando, que el signor iva a apareser con la plata, ma en lougar de paras, foé que vimos aparesser 2 officieres de la Armada Franceza i 2 de la Aramada Inglesa, i mos empessaron à demandar, "coantos dedos tiené el tourco en cada pié," coantas naves tiené, coantos soldados coantas naves tiené, coantos soldados canones, onde estan situados, i tantas otras cozas que no me interessavan, porqué yo queria moneda "that's all." Le respondi que yo era "zera de lenyo," que no savia nada, que yo lo que queria era paras, i la repoesta foé ouna pounta de pied.

No me recuerdo la data que quitimos Metelin, ma loqué estouvimos foe 5 dias, i partimos para Pereo, en oun vapor

identifying us as Frenchmen. After making us wait about half an hour, he told us that we were allowed to disembark.

Once on land, we went to the barber, because our beards had grown into knotted bundles. Then we went to the hotel, where we slept until 11 in the morning. We ate a little, and right away we sent you a telegram saying we had arrived.

My first order of business was to look for the French consul and coax some money out of him. We found him, and I explained our problems. He was Greek and didn't even speak French. He told us repeatedly that he had no authority to spend even a penny on behalf of the French government and therefore could not help us. But finally, after I broke my head to get something from him and bored him to death with my repeated tale of woe, he told us, to get rid of me, that he was prepared to give us a letter to the shipping company for our free passage to Piraeus, second class, and that it was not possible to give us money. He also gave us a letter of recommendation to a charitable organization in Mytilene that would probably help us.

Why lose a minute? We went there and showed them the letter, which they forwarded to the person to whom it was addressed. We were waiting for the gentleman to appear with the money, but instead of money there appeared two officers of the French army and two of the English army. They began asking us how many toes a Turk has on each foot, how many ships he has, how many soldiers, and so many other things that were of no interest to me, because all I wanted was money, *that's all*! I replied that I was as dense as a block of wood, that I knew nothing, that what I wanted was money. The answer I got was a kick in the behind.

I don't remember the date we left Mytilene, but we were there for five days. We left for Piraeus on a Greek ship that weighed 250 tons—imagine how huge that ship was!

Grego, de 250 tonelatas, imaginadvos la grandor "Boy de ouna barquita." De Metelin mos foimos a Chio, i pasimos oun v agé el mas agradavlé porqué la mar estava calma. Salimos aï en Chio i estouvimos aï oun dia (Ermozo lougar).

El viagé de Chio a Pereo foe mouy terriblé, fortuna louvia pidrisco, el Dio se arto de azer todo loque quijo. No mos quedo tripas, 40 passageros todos medios moertos. Yo queria mostrar, que no me espantava, sali al Ponté, me qualli, i me cuitï los meoyos. "Ouna mas en la tinia de Efraimico!" Lo que paresia que cada minouto mos ivamos a oundir, esto era la rotché.

Ala maniana que esperavamos, troco en el tiempo, "Good right shirt," era mas negro que la notché passada. Enfin ya arivimos a Pereo, yo con ouna riza colorada atada en la frenté dela caïda que me cayi, Albert estava lavado, de tanto goumitar. Todos los 2 lo que aprestavamos era para el esierco, ma grassias a Dios ya estavamos bivos.

From Mytilene we went to Chios. We had a most pleasant trip because the sea was calm. We got off in Chios—beautiful place.

The trip from Chios to Piraeus was terrible—storm, rain, hail. God had a field day, doing whatever He wished. Our stomachs were gone . . . 40 passengers, all half dead. I wanted to show that I wasn't afraid, so I went out onto the bridge. I fell down and knocked my brains out—one more sore on Efraimiko's[6] mangy scalp, as if he didn't have enough! Every minute it looked as if we would sink. That was the night.

In the morning, which we were anxiously awaiting, the weather changed (*Good night shirt*)[7]—it was worse than the night before. We did finally arrive in Piraeus, I with a red handkerchief tied around my forehead because of my fall, and Albert cleaned out from vomiting so much. The two of us were fit to be thrown into the garbage, but thank God we were still alive.

6. Diminuitive for comic effect

7. A possible reference to Thomas Hood's poem *The Song of the Shirt* (1843), in which a woman sings of her miserable existence, forever working on the shirt, through tears and hunger. This poem also refers to "the Barbarous Turk."

passi dizde que quiti Smyrna
la mar no me tomo mientres el
viage ma de ver ombres mujeres
criaturas yorando, gritando, quien
con la pataya, quien con talet i
Tifilin, i me azia tanto pena fin
que yo tambien me metia a yorar
enfin despues de un tan negro
viage arivimos a New York
el 26 december, onde no pudimos
desparcer siendo que era el
dia dela fiesta de Noël, al dia
siguiente, mos tomaron del vapor
a un vapor tchico, (esto azen
solo a los passajeros de 3ª classa)
i mos yevaron a (Elis Island)
or (Castel Garden) por examinar
los ojos i los cuerpos, si saviamos
muldar i escribir, enfin despues
de ir de un bureau a otro, i
sin ninguna dificultad mos
decharon entrar en los Estados
... en ... lugar ... Island

Facsimile of a left-facing interior page
from the original *Diario*

Facsimile of a right-facing interior page
from the original *Diario*

Parté 2

Ouna vez debarcados al pasaporto i despoes de mountchas
dificultades las otoridades mos decharon entrar en el Païs. La
primera coza foe irmos al Hotel i repozarmos oun poco, enfin
aquel dia i la notché no salimos del Hotel. Ala maniana la
primera coza que dessidimos a azer, foé pircourar a encontrar
algounos de moestros sivdadinos, residiendo en Pireaus, i
grassias al propretario del hotel, mos indico onde podriamos
encontrar algounos.

I ansi foimos à esté café i a moestro encanto la primera
persona que encontrimos foe el Signor Moïse Alalouf,
Importador i Exportador de Smyrna. Verdadmenté no vos
poedo explicar con pendola, la mouy generoza bienvenida,
que este signor Alalouf mos acordo. Despoes de conversar
con el por ounos coantos momentos, explicandomos las
condisionés del Païs, i mos convensio que no podiamos azer
nada aï, quero dizir no podiamos mentenermos, porque los
etchos estavan mouy calmos. Enfin, mozotros sigoun ya
savech no teniamos idea de estabilssirmos aï, i esperavamos
que la gera acavaria en oun courto tiempo, i retornarmos a
Smyrna. La maniana la passimos en este café, mientres ke
despoes de medio dia mos passimos oun poco en el Quais.

La notché, despoes de senar, mos foïmos del hotel de
boena ora, por discoutir, que deviamos azer, por lavorar, i
ganar alo menos noestros gastes diaryos. Discoutiendo con
Albert pensi que era ouna boena idea, ir onde el Consolato
Frances, i contaldé moestros dertes. Dounqué desidimos,
que ala maniana procsima, sin piedrer tiempo, ivamos a ver
al Consul.

Part II

Once we had disembarked at the port of call, the authorities, after many difficulties, let us enter the country. The first thing we did was go to the hotel and rest a little. So that day and night we didn't leave the hotel. The next morning we decided, first thing, to meet some of our fellow citizens who lived in Piraeus. Thanks to the owner of the hotel, who told us where we could find them!

So we went to that café, and, to our delight, the first person we met was Mr. Moïse Alalouf, importer and exporter from Smyrna. Truly, I cannot convey to you with my pen the very generous welcome that this Mr. Alalouf accorded us. We talked with him for some time, and he explained to us the conditions in the country, trying to convince us that we could not do anything there to support ourselves because work was very scarce. Of course, as you know, we had no intention of settling there. We hoped that the war would end after a short time, and that we would return to Smyrna. We spent the morning in the café, and in the afternoon we took a little walk along the quay.

That night, after dinner, we returned to the hotel early to discuss what we had to do to work and earn at least enough for our daily expenses. Discussing it with Albert, I thought it would be a good idea to go to the French consul and tell him our troubles. We decided that, not to lose any time, we would go to see the consul the next morning.

Ansi foe, i alas 8:30 dela maniana mos topimos en e bureau del Consul i esperimos fin las 9:30 fin que vino. Entrimos asou bureau. Despoes de presentar noestros papeles i passaportos le diché como vinimos a Pireaus, que no conosiamos a ninguno, i que por consigoenté no podiamos encontrar lavoro, porqué no avlavamos la lingua, i que podriamos mourir de ambré si algouno no mos ayoudava. Despoes de tanto rogarlé porque se enteressara en nozotros, nos prometio que al dia siguiente, iva a ver al Ambassador en Athènes, i que iva a pircourar a azer algo por nozotros. I yo para travarlé mas la goaya (Excusad mi espression) le diché que no teniamos ni oun sintavo por comer, ansi que por dormir, i despoes de hezitar oun poco, mos dio a 20 francos a cada ouno, por los dias fin que aranjava algouna coza con el Ambassador. Dounque esto ya foe oun boen empessijo, eh?

Estos dos dias los passimos, oun poco mas alegres que los dias passados, i mos passeimos en el porto, i foïmos a Athènes, en compania del signor Alalouf i otro signor.

El dia vino onde ivamos a saver algo del Consul. Foïmos aï temprano (First thing in the morning), i mos dicho que malorozamente no pudo azer nada con el Ambassador, i que calia que nozotros nos presentaramos en persona onde el secretario dela ambassada, i que le explicaramos todo. Le demandi si era menester aranjar pour ouna entrevista. Mos dicho que calia i para esto calia escrivir ouna letra al Ambassador demandando por ouna entrevista siendo se tratava de ouna question de emportansa. Esto no manqui de azer imediatamenté. Le escrivi, i al otro dia ressivimos la reboesta, que podiamos ver a sou secretario en la embassada. Sin piedrer tiempo tomimos el treno para Athenes i mos izimos conduisir ala Ambassada.

Antes de entrar, desidimos que aï era la oltima chance que teniamos por obtener algo de ayoudo, i que para parvenir a algo, calia avlar i mountcho, falsear sin carar, por todo

And so we did. At 8:30 in the morning we were in the consul's office, and we waited until he arrived, at 9:30. We went into his office, and, after presenting our papers and passports, told him how we came to Piraeus, that we didn't know anybody, that we couldn't find work because we didn't know the language, and that we could die of hunger if someone didn't help us. After we pleaded with him so much, so he would take an interest in us, he promised us that the following day he would see the ambassador in Athens and try to do something for us. In order to pull more at his 'heartstrings'[8] —excuse the expression—I told him that we didn't even have a dime to eat or sleep. After hesitating a little, he gave us each 20 francs to tide us over until he could arrange something with the ambassador. This was a good beginning, *eh?*

Those two days we spent a little happier than the previous ones. We took a walk around the port and went to Athens, accompanied by Mr. Alalouf and another gentleman.

The day we were supposed to hear from the consul arrived. We went there early, *first thing in the morning.* He told us that, unfortunately, he could do nothing with the ambassador. He advised us to present ourselves in person to the secretary of the embassy and explain everything. I asked him if it was necessary to arrange for an interview. He said that it was, indeed, and that we should write a letter to the ambassador requesting an interview because it was a matter of importance. I wrote him immediately, and the next day we received the reply that we could see his secretary at the embassy. Without losing a minute, we took the train to Athens and asked for directions to the embassy.

Before entering, we decided that this would be the last chance we had to get any help, and that to get anything, we would have to talk as much as we could, exaggerate without limit what we had suffered, and even cry if need be. So we went in. We had to wait about 2 hours to see this gentleman,

8. Actual reference is to the male organ!

ʿoque soufreïmos, i si se necesitava mizmo yorar, calia yorado. Enfin entrimos, i touvimos que esperar como 2 oras para ver a este signor, i mos izo yamar a sou bureau, i sin alargarvos mountcho en las questiones, i las repoestas, que exgengimos, le expliqui todo, i con sou demazia todas las sufriensas i enconviniensas que touvimos dizdé que deshimos Smyrna, i todo lo que podiamos devenir, si no mos acordava sous ayudo, o si no mos topava oun empiego, i ganar moestra vida fin que la Guerra se acavava. A esto mos respondio que la embassada no era "Agence d'employement" i que por consigoenté no mos podia topar ningun travajo, i mos dicho que todo loqué podian azer, ya mo lo iva azer saver mezo el Consul en Pireaus, el dia siguienté. Salimos de aï con la esperansa de resivir ouna repoesta favorable mezo el Consul.

Dounqué al dia siguienté que se menea de aï? Esperando sous repoesta, en el Consolato, coando ya vino el Consul i mos izo yamar, i mos dicho que el Ambassador desidio en noestra favor i que ivamos a ressivir 200 francos al mez por los 2 por moestra estada en Grecia i que esta souma la ivamos a ressivir mezzo el Consul a 100 francos todos los 15 dias. Agora quedava la question, si ivamos aser pagados ala Anglé o a la tourca, i grasias a Dios que ya foé ala Anglé. 200 frs. ya vos imaginach que no abasta para 2 personas al mez, i pensimos que la onica coza era azer la economia, i para empessar, qualia deshado el hotel, i bouchcado ouna camareta, con algouna familia Grega, i esto foe lo que izimos.

Topimos ouna camareta, con pagar 15 francos al mez, ma la camareta era ouna couzina vazia, ma conteniendo ouna cama armada, sin coltchon o coltcha etc, i calia mercado estas todas cozas. Pensimos que mas convenia mercar estas cozas que de pagar 5 francos al dia por el hotel. Dounque merquimos estas cozas, i ya atacanimos la cama, sigoun foe ya mos passimos mouy boenos.

until he called us into his office. I won't tell you all the questions and answers, but I did explain everything and more, all the suffering and hardship we had endured since leaving Smyrna, and what could become of us if he did not grant us his assistance or did not find us some work so we could earn a living until the war ended. To this he replied that the embassy was not an employment agency, and that he could therefore not find us a job. He told us that whatever he could do would be made known to us by the consul in Piraeus the following day. We left there with the hope of receiving a favorable reply through the consul.

So why even budge from there the following day? We were waiting for his reply at the consulate, when the consul himself came and called us in and told us that the ambassador had decided in our favor. We were to receive 200 francs a month for the two of us during our stay in Greece, and we would receive this amount through the consul, 100 francs every 15 days. Now the question remained whether we would be paid in the English way or the Turkish way [meaning not clear]. Thank God it was in the English way. You can imagine that 200 francs was not enough for two people to live on for a month. We decided that the only thing to do was to economize, and, for a start, to leave the hotel and look for a room with a Greek family. This is what we did.

We found a room for 15 francs a month, but the room was an empty kitchen with an army bed, with no mattress, no blanket, etc., so we had to buy all these things. We decided that it was better for us to buy these things than to pay 5 francs a day for the hotel. So we bought these things, and we fixed up the bed. As it turned out, we got along very well.

La signora de caza naturalmente grega, i emperegada,
nr a ya mos queria bien, siendo que le dichimos que eramos
francezes, i mos metio al enclavado (Hristos) enriva en
el canton dela pared i todas las manianas, mos trocava la
coupa de azëite i la metcha, ke ensendia alado del hristos. Ya
vɔs azech ouna idea las bodas i las comedias que teniamos
tɵdas las notches coando mos ivamos a dourmir teniendo al
eɹclavado enriva de mozotros, i que la signora no se olvidava
a acodrarmos todas las notchés aque no olvidemos a rogar
pɔr la panaya i el hristos. No quedavamos de reir, coando
lɵ mas delas manianas venia con el haber que se sogno por
rɵozotros, i dizia que via ala mama en la eglisia, rogando por
rɵozotros, i que el hristos se desclavava i bezava a la mama, i le
prometia que el ya estava teniendo cargo de sous ijos. No era
esto mijor de Theatro?

Por no alargar mountcho sovré moestra estada en Grecia,
vɵs dire que los Dias los passavamos en passearmos en
cɵmpania del signor Alalouf o con otros i las notchés mos
cɵrmiamos de mouy demprano, siempré esperando la fin dela
guera. Ansi passimos de August fin November, coando en los
primeros dias de November por hazardo encontrimos a oun
Signor de Salonique (djoudio) i sou nombre es Leon Magriso.
Lo encontrimos en el Restorant que comiamos. Despoes de
entroducirmos de parte a parte, i entrando en conversasion,
mos izo saver que el iva a partir para los Estados Unidos de
America, i esperava en Pireaus por vapor.

Sin alargar sovre este sojeto, esté Signor Magriso, me
se izo tanto amigo que no passava dia que no boushcava à
vermé, siempre avlando por sou viajé alos Estados Unidos.
Tanto mos enterissimos ouno del otro, fin que me propozo
a partir con el, yo sigoun ya vos imajinach, no tenia idea del
todo a quitar la Grecia, que siempré esperava la fin dela guera,
por retornar a Smyrna. Dounqué viendo el coantidad que
me forsava, le diché que podria tomar sou propozision en

The lady of the house was, naturally, Greek, and a housemaid, but she liked us, since we told her that we were Frenchmen. She hung a crucifix[9] for us up above in the corner of the wall, and every morning she changed the cup of oil and the wick that she lit next to the crucifix. You can imagine the amusement[10] that we had every night when we went to sleep with the crucifix above us. And every night, without fail, the lady reminded us to pray to the Virgin Mary and to Christ. We couldn't stop laughing when she came, as she did most mornings, with the news that she dreamed about us—she would see the mama in the church praying for us, and Christ would uncrucify himself and kiss his mama, and would promise her that he was, indeed, taking care of his children. Wasn't that better than the theater?

Not to go on too long about our stay in Greece, I'll tell you that we spent the days taking walks with Mr. Alalouf and others and went to sleep very early, always hoping for the end of the war. Thus passed the time from *August* until *November*. In the first days of *November* we met, by chance, a gentleman from Salonika, a Jew. His name was Leon Magriso. We met him in the restaurant where we ate. After we had all introduced ourselves and started a conversation, he told us that he was going to leave for the United States of America, and that he was waiting for the ship in Piraeus.

I won't say more on this subject, but this Mr. Magriso became such a close friend that a day didn't pass that he didn't seek me out, always talking about his voyage to the United States. We became so interested in each other that he proposed that I leave with him. As you can imagine, the idea of leaving Greece had never occurred to me, for, as always, I was hoping for the end of the war so I could return to Smyrna. He forced this idea on me so much that I told him I would take his proposition into consideration, with two conditions. First, I had to talk with Albert because I didn't want to leave

9. Literally, "the nailed one (Christ)"
10. Literally, "weddings and comedies"

ccnsideration, en 2 conditiones, la ouna que calia avlar con Albert, porque no queria partir solo, i sigunda, porqué no tenia fondos bastanté para comprar bilieto i calia que me ayoudava el (Magriso). Para esto me dicho que el iva azer todo sou possiblé a ayoudarme ami solo, i pagarlé en arivando ala America.

Enfin ala notché avli con Albert i discoutiendo el projeto, siempré mos descorajavamos a venir ala America por mountchas razones, principalmenté por no saver la lingua. Dounque aquea notché no durmimos, pensando alo ke deviamos azer fin que desidimos a partir, con el entendimiento que este signor me iva ayoudar a pagar ouna partida del bilieto.

Ala maniana encontri a este amigo i le diché que ya desidimos a partir con el, i se alegro mountcho. En mientres passo ounos coantos dias indo al doctor a egsaminarmos los ojos.

Coando ya mos empessimos a aprontarmos a partir, i que lo que mancava era visar el passaporto i mercar el bilieto, esto era ouna semana antes de partir, oun dia no encontrando a este amigo, foimos a sou hotel, a demandar por el, coando el proprietario del hotel mos izo saver que el signor estava bien hasino i foe ovligado a yamar ouna ambulansa i lo mando al hospital. De vista mos apressurimos al hospital i saver de el, dounque lo vimos, i el doctor en el hospital mos dicho que soufria del Apendecite i que qualia operado, i ouna vez operado, calia que se repozara alo menos oun mez, por comportar oun tan longo viajé.

Dounque ya vos imaginach como todos moestros planes se foeron al agoa, por el momento, ma nozotros que ya mos desidimos a partir costa lo que costa, dishimos que calia bouchcado otros remedios, por obtener fondos, i adjustar a lo poco que teniamos, (los bilietos costavan a 450 francos por ouno en tresera classa). Dounque pensimos, si mos

alone, and second, because I didn't have sufficient funds to buy a ticket, he (Magriso) would have to help me. He said he would do everything in his power to help me—only me, and I could pay him when we got to America.

So that night I spoke with Albert. Discussing the project, we remained hesitant about coming to America for many reasons, above all because we didn't know the language. That night we didn't sleep, wondering what we should do, until we decided to leave, with the understanding that this gentleman would help me pay for part of the ticket.

In the morning, I met this friend and told him that we had decided to leave with him, and he was very pleased. We spent several days going to the doctor to have our eyes examined.

After we had started preparing for the trip—the only things left were to visa our passports and buy the tickets—this was a week before we were set to leave, one day, when we didn't meet this friend as usual, we went to his hotel to ask for him. The owner of the hotel informed us that the gentleman was quite ill, and that he had had to call an ambulance to bring him to the hospital. Right away we rushed to the hospital. We saw him, and the doctor in the hospital told us that he was suffering from appendicitis and would have to be operated on. After the operation, he would need to rest for at least a month in order to endure such a long voyage.

You can imagine how all our plans went down the drain for the moment, but we had already decided to leave, whatever the cost. We had to look for other ways to obtain funds to add to the little we had (the tickets cost 450 francs apiece, third class). If we could find the courage, we thought we would go to the French consul and ask if it would be possible for them to send us to America at their expense. The next day was the day we were to receive the 100 francs, so we went there. Before telling him about our situation, we took the money and signed, as usual, to confirm receipt of that sum.

encorajavamos a ir i demandar al Consul Frances si era possible, a mandarmos Ala America a sous gastes, i el procsimo dia era el dia onde resiviamos la quinzena, i foïmos aï. Antes de avlarlé, por moestro dert, tomimos las halacas, i siempre signavamos ouna resivida por la souma que ressiviamos. Despoes le demandi si le podia avlar, ounos coantos minoutos, i mos dicho que no tenia tiempo, i que foeramos el mizmo dia despoes de la medio dia.

Ansi foé, despoes de medio dia foi yo solo, i le diché como pensavamos partir para los Estados Unidos, por no topar lavora aï en Grecia, i mos avergoensavamos siempre todas las vezes que ivamos a ressivir la pension, que el governo Frances era tan boeno i generozo a acordarmos i enfin mountchas otras cozas. Despoes de explicarmé, me dicho, que esto era impossiblé, i que por consigoensa, no mos podia acordar ni oun centime para irmos ala America, i mos dicho que el Ambassador mos acordo esta pension todo tiempo que estamos en Grecia, sin lavorar.

I mas mos dicho, que mos acordaria passaje en sigounda classa en ouna de los primeros vapores que partiria, si queriamos partir para la França, i ayoudar a moestra Patria. I yo le diché, despoes de rengrassiarlo, por todo esto, que nozotros estavamos prontos a irmos a Francia i ayoudar ala Patria, si la Francia mos reconosia por verdaderos Francezes (Citoyen Français) i que la onica razon que no queriamos partir para la Francia era por el prejudicio, que eramos protegés Français, i sovre todo nassido en Tourquia, i que los Francezes en Francia aboressian los protegés Francezes, nassidos en Tourquia, i no tenian la confiensa en eyos, sigoun letras que ressivimos de moestros amigos.

Dounque ya entendech que lo que conti esta hestoria, foé para escaparla de el, porque lo tenia menester, para que me signara alo menos el passaporto que sin vizar el passaporto

Then I asked if we could speak with him for a few minutes. He said he didn't have time and we should come back later that day, after noon.

So in the afternoon I went alone, and I told him how we were thinking of leaving for the United States because we couldn't find work in Greece, how ashamed we were every time we went to get the stipend that the French government was so kind and generous to grant us, and many other things as well. After I had explained all this, he told me that it was impossible. He could not grant us even one "centime" to go to America. The ambassador, he said, is granting us this stipend the whole time we are in Greece without working.

He also told us that the ambassador would grant us passage, second class, in one of the first ships to leave, if we wished to leave for France and help our homeland. After thanking him for all this, I told him that we would be ready to go to France and help the homeland if France recognized us as true Frenchmen (French citizens), and that the only reason we did not wish to leave for France was because of the prejudice against French subjects, especially those born in Turkey. The French in France detested French subjects born in Turkey, and they did not trust them, according to letters we received from our friends.

You do understand that I told him this story to placate him, because I needed him so he could at least sign our passports—without this we could not leave. I kept on speaking to him, until he told me that he could do nothing for us beyond signing our passports.

When we saw that there was not the slightest hope there, we went to seek other solutions. Two days passed without doing anything, and we were short 300 francs. Meanwhile, Mr. Magriso had left the hospital. We met with him, and he told me that he could not leave for two or three months,

no podia partir, i tanto le avli, fin que me dicho que no podia azer nada por nozotros solo que signar noestro passaporto.

Dounque coando vimos, que de aï no avia la mas tchica esperansa, mos foimos por bouchcar otros remedios, 2 dias mas passaron sin azer nada, i mos mancava como 300 francos. El signor Magriso en mientres quito el hospital i lo encontrimos, i me dicho, que el no podia partir por dos o tres mezes, siendo que no se sintia boeno, i que regretava no poder ayoudarmé. Despoes de 3-4 dias de ir por aqui i por aï, siempré en compania del signor Alalouf, coando ouna demaniana, Albert encontro oun amigo de Rhodes, i tenia de vender oun barco de sevoya, i no poudiendolo venderlo le dicho a Albert que bouchcar a venderlo, con commission. Grassias que Albert vendio el barco de sevoya para poder remediarmos a partir.

Despues de prepararmos todo como bilietos i vizitas medicales i otras cozas, partimos el 26 november por New York con vapor grego "Joanina." En dos dias arivimos a Patras. Despoes de estar ai 24 oras partimos para Algiers (Africa). Arivados a Africa despoes de 8 dias de malo tiempo que no soupimos lo que es dourmir por mas peor estavamos en 3d classa. El vapor tomo carvon aï por 48 i los passajeros no foeron autorizados a salir a tierra, porqué avia malatia en el lougar. Por darvos ouna idea lo que es este magnifico porto, vos dire que el lougar no es mouy grande, ma bien fragoada, i artisticamente adonado con parcos por todas las partes. El Quais paresse joustamente como el de Smyrna i la climat es deliciozo.

De Algiers partimos el 3 December, con oun tiempo magnifico, que touro solo por 2-3 dias. El resto del viagé lo passimos lo mas malo que se poede imaginar. No bastava las tempestas, i negros tiempos solo, i qualia espantarmos de submarinos Almanes que eran mouy nombrozos por aqueas mares—2 dias antes de arivar a Gibraltar, el vapor foe

since he was not feeling well. He was sorry he could not help me. We spent 3 or 4 days going here and there, always accompanied by Mr. Alalouf. Then, one morning, Albert met a friend from Rhodes who had to sell a shipload of onions. Unable to sell it himself, he asked Albert to try to sell it, promising him a commission. Thanks to Albert's success in selling the shipload of onions, we could now leave.

After attending to and preparing all that was necessary, like tickets and medical visits and other things, we left for New York on November 26 on the ship Joanina. After two days we arrived in Patras. After staying there 24 hours, we left for Algiers (Africa). We arrived in Africa after 8 days of bad weather—we didn't know what sleep was. Being in third class made it even worse. The ship loaded coal there for 48 hours, and the passengers were not authorized to disembark because there was disease in the place. To give you an idea of this magnificent port, I will tell you that the place is not very big, but nicely laid out and artistically and generously adorned with parks. The quay looks exactly like the quay in Smyrna, and the climate is delicious.

We left Algiers *December* 3 in magnificent weather, which lasted only 2-3 days. The rest of the trip we spent in the worst way imaginable. As if the storms and harsh weather weren't enough, we had to watch out for German submarines, which were very numerous in those seas. Two days before arriving in Gibraltar, the ship was forced to stop per order of a German submarine. As the submarine was coming closer to the ship, all our hearts were pounding, for we didn't know what was to become of us. When the submarine was alongside the ship, it ordered the captain of the ship to send an officer to board the submarine, bringing a list of the cargo and a list of passengers. To come to the point, after half an hour the officer returned, and we were allowed to depart.

o-ligado a quedarse por orden de oun submarino Alman. El submarino a mizoura que asercava del vapor, los corassones de todos batian que no savian qualo iva a devinir de todos. Enfin al submarino ouna vez alado del vapor, ordeno al capitan del vapor a que mandara oun officier a bordo del sabmarino, con el manifesto dela carga i la lista de passajeros. Dounque sin alargar sovre esto, despoes de 1/2 ora el oficier retorno, i foimos permetidos a partir.

Ala notché arivimos a Gibraltar, i mos ordenaron a enchorar aï por la notché. Ala maniana, 2 officieres vinieron a bordo a egzaminar los manifesto, i a todos los passajeros individoualmente. Aquea maniana mizma partimos por New York directamente.

Por el tiempo no vo lo quereria escrivir, porque me va a cavzar mountcha pena si me acodro de todas las oras malas que passimos de Gibraltar a New York. Mientres el viagé ouna notché el tiempo estava tanto negro, que el vapor estava adelantando a 3 milias la ora por 3-4 oras. Despoes el tiempo deviniendo mas negro, abacho el Capitan i mos dicho que el tiempo se iva azer tanto negro que avia miedo, i mos izo dar coedras para atarmos en las camas, i ansi lo izimos. Despoes de ouna ora la tempesta devino tanto negra que la agoa estava entrando por los olouques del vapor. La notché entera estouvo lo mizmo sin trocar i grassias a Dios que ala maniana troco oun poco i soupimos que el vapor en lougar de adelantar se foe 350 milias atras.

En verdad aquea notché foe ouna delas mas malas notches que passi dizdé que quiti Smyrna. La mar no me tomo mientres el viagé ma de ver ombres moujeres criatouras yorando, gritando, quen con la panaya, quen con talet i tifilin, i me azia tanto pena fin que yo tambien me meti a yorar.

Enfin despoes de oun tan negro viagé arivimos a New York el 25 december, onde no poudimos desbarcar siendo que era el dia dela fiesta de Noël. Al dia siguiente, mos tomaron

That night we arrived in Gibraltar, and they ordered us to lay anchor there for the night. In the morning two officers came on board to examine the lists and all the passengers individually. That same morning we left directly for New York.

About the weather I hesitate to write you, because it will be very painful for me to remember all the terrible hours we spent from Gibraltar to New York. One night during the trip the weather was so bad that the ship was advancing 3 miles an hour for 3-4 hours. When the weather got worse, the captain came down and told us that it threatened to become so bad that there were serious concerns. He ordered that we be given ropes to tie ourselves up in our beds, and so we did. After an hour the storm became so severe that water was coming in through the drainpipes of the ship. The whole night it stayed the same, without changing. Thank God it changed a little in the morning, and we learned that instead of advancing, the ship had gone 350 miles back.

Indeed, that night was one of the worst nights that I spent since I left Smyrna. The sea did not claim me during the voyage, but to see men, women, children, crying, screaming, some with the Virgin Mary, others with *tallit* and *tefillin* [Jewish prayer garment and phylacteries]—it pained me so much that I also started to cry.

Finally, after such a terrible voyage, we arrived in New York *December* 25. We could not disembark because it was the Christmas holiday. The next day they transferred us from the ship to a small ship (they do this only with passengers from third class), and they brought us to Ellis Island *or* Castle Garden to examine our eyes and bodies and determine whether we could read and write.

del vapor aoun vapor tchico (esto azen solo alos passajeros de 3d classa), i mos yevaron a Elis Island or Castel Garden por egzaminarmos los ojos i los coerpos, si saviamos meldar i escrivir.

Enfin despoes de ir de oun bureau a otro, i sin ningouna dificultad mos decharon entrar en los Estados Unidos. Este lougar Elis Island es una isla, de manera que qualia tomado oun vapor para ir a New York, i ya vos imaginach, yo i Albert que no saviamos ni Ba ni Bou qualia topar el lougar, mientres que todos los immigrantes tienen aqui algouno que los van aressivir i no tienen pena.

I por acavar vos diré que topimos el lougar i vinimos a New York i estouvimos batal por oun tiempo i topimos etcho i todo mos se izo colay. I estamos mouy ventourozos, siendo que Albert se cazo i esta boeno, i yo Alfred que mi novia me esperava aqui por 24 anios, i sercamente me cazaré i espero ser ventourozo. Con esto do mil grassias a Dios i a los Estados Unidos que me salvaron poedo dizir la vida.

I mizmo que malorozamente tan lechos de vozotros quiridos, i esto sigouro regretach por no poder vermé, aouncontodo alegradvos que esto bivo despoes de todo lo que passi. I biviré para servos siempre ijo i ermano quirido i para nounca olvidarvos i con la esperansa de vervos sercamenté quedo como siempre lo fuï voestro quirido devoado i inoulvidavlé ijo i hermano

Finally, after going from one office to another, we were allowed to enter the United States without any difficulty. This place, Ellis Island, is an island, so you have to go to New York by boat. As you can imagine, Albert and I didn't know from nothing. We had to find the place, unlike other immigrants, who have someone here to receive them and have no trouble.

To conclude, I will tell you that we did find the place and come to New York. We were unemployed for a while, but we did find work, and everything ran smoothly for us. We are very lucky, since Albert got married and is well, and as for me, Alfred, my bride was waiting here for me for 24 years, and I will soon be getting married, and I am hoping for good luck. And so I give a thousand thanks to God and to the United States—I can say that they saved my life.

Even if I am, unfortunately, so far away from you dear ones, and I am sure that you are sorry that you can't see me, still, in spite of everything, be happy that I am alive after all I went through. As long as I live I will always be your dear son and brother, and I will never forget you. With the hope of seeing all of you soon, I remain, as I always was, your dear, devoted and unforgettable son and brother,

Alfred

Alfred Ascher in his later years, 1978-86,
Worcester, Massachusetts. Courtesy of Robert Ascher

Facsimile of the original *Diario's* final page

About the Authors

Alfred Ascher was born in Smyrna, now Izmir, Turkey in 1892 to Yakov and Rachel (Rosa) Arditti Ascher. He attended the Alliance Israélite Universelle school in Smyrna, and, like his older brother, Albert, was a French citizen—dangerous in Turkey during World War I. They escaped from Turkey in 1915 to wait out the war in Greece, but eventually left for New York. There Alfred met and married Claire Eliscu. They were blessed with two children, Lorraine and Robert, and the family settled in Far Rockaway, NY. After serving as head supervisor for steamship companies in New York, Alfred retired to St. Petersburg, Florida. Claire died in 1949. Alfred's second wife, Beatrice Brean, died in or before 1978. In that year he moved to Worcester, Massachusetts, near his daughter. Alfred Ascher died on January, 26th, 1986, leaving a legacy of devotion, generosity, courage, and fun.

Gloria J. Ascher was born in the Bronx, New York to Emanuel and Esther (Ganon) Ascher, Ladino-speaking Sephardic Jews from Smyrna, now Izmir, Turkey. She attended the Bronx H.S. of Science, Hunter College, the University of Bonn (Fulbright Grant), and Yale University. As Associate Professor (now Emerita) of German, Scandinavian and Judaic Studies and founding Co-director of Judaic Studies at Tufts University, she taught Ladino Language and Culture on all levels, beginning with an introductory course in January, 2000, through May, 2017—the first regularly offered, substantially enrolled Ladino courses at a U.S. college or university. She prepared English editions of Matilda Koén-Sarano's Ladino textbooks for beginners and advanced students, and has written and presented on Ladino and Sephardic subjects, and on Old Norse and German literature. She sings and composes songs and writes poems in Ladino, and teaches the language independently.